# Western Visions:
## Perspectives on the West in Canada

# Western Visions:
# Perspectives on the West in Canada.

Roger Gibbins and Sonia Arrison

broadview press

**Canadian Cataloguing in Publication Data**

Gibbins, Roger, 1947-
  Western visions

Includes index
ISBN 1-55111-073-3

1. Canada Western—Politics and government.
2. Canada—Politics and government—1993-
I. Arrison, Sonia, 1972-    II. Title.


FC3219.G52   1995   971.20'3   C95-932568-9
F1060.92.G52   1995


Broadview Press
Post Office Box 1243, Peterborough, Ontario, Canada K9J 7H5

in the United States of America:
3576 California Road, Orchard Park, NY 14127

in the United Kingdom:
B.R.A.D. Book Representation & Distribution Ltd.,
244A London Road, Hadleigh, Essex. SS7 2DE


PRINTED IN CANADA

# Table of Contents

# Acknowledgements

This work draws from an extensive body of existing scholarship that is recognized only in part through citations and references. We would therefore like to acknowledge the debt we owe to the community of Western Canadian political scholars. More specifically, we would like to thank Nelson Wiseman, and Linda Trimble, whose critical comments on a draft manuscript were of immense assistance. Jodi Cockerill provided very useful research and commentary on the Saskatchewan scene, Peter Stoyko provided the same from Manitoba, Judi Powell turned rough ideas into striking graphics, Heather Bala handled the difficult indexing task, and Valerie Snowdon cheerfully processed one draft after another. Finally, we would like to thank the Social Sciences and Humanities Research Council of Canada (Grant 410-92-0276), whose program funding supported many of the research costs associated with this project.

# CHAPTER ONE

# A Community Under Stress

"The West," like many regional communities, takes on greater coherence and homogeneity the farther away one moves. The closer you get to the land and its people, the more the region begins to fragment into quite distinctive provincial communities, and then fragment again into a multitude of other communities within the provinces themselves. No one, for example, would confuse Regina with Vancouver or, within British Columbia, Prince George with Victoria. Thus to view the West up close is like looking into a kaleidoscope in which the brightly coloured pieces overwhelm the regional pattern. And yet, despite often competing interests and sharply etched community differences, the West maintains some degree of coherence and some reasonable measure of distinctiveness from other regional communities in Canada. Both the regional glue and distinctiveness, we would suggest, come less from the region's varied geography and more from how Western Canadians see the world, and particularly the political world. In Richard Allen's evocative phrase, the West is "a region of the mind,"[1] and this is the region we will explore in the chapters to come.

Our emphasis throughout will be on the *political* themes and tensions that have characterized the region, helped tie it together and, at times, set it apart from the larger Canadian community. More specifically, the emphasis will be on *national* visions and sentiment within the West. But does it make sense to talk about nationalism in a regional context? Are we not talking about regionalism? Or, more alarmingly, are we talking about an emergent nationalism that is not Canadian at all, that looks toward a new national community beginning at the Ontario—Manitoba border, or perhaps even farther west? Does nationalism within the Western Canadian context refer primarily to a deep sense of commitment to Canada, or does it serve to capture the chronic tension that has existed between the West and the broader Canadian community?

By nationalism, we mean first a strong identification with a place—a specific territorial community—and its people, an emotional attachment that is perhaps most strongly associated with the term *patriotism*. However, nationalism also entails a political road map. It provides a set of symbols, guideposts, and interpretative fables which shape political perceptions and behaviours, and identify both heroes and villains. And third, nationalism encompasses not only a shared sense of the past but a positive vision of the future. It is in this last sense that we can talk about a "national vision." To date, the territorial community that has been the focal point of nationalism in the West has been *Canada*, and not the region itself. National visions in Western Canada have been shaped by the regional experience, but their emotional centre has been found in the country at large and not in the West. Thus the founding (and now discarded) slogan of the Reform party—"the West wants in!"—captures the traditional essence of Western Canadian nationalism. However, the emotional centre for national sentiment in the West could shift, and it is by no means beyond the realm of possibility that it could shift to the region and perhaps even to provincial communities within the region. Canada is in a state of flux as we address fiscal constraints and the challenges posed by sovereigntists in Quebec, and it is by no means clear that the country will evolve in line with western visions and interests. Therefore we cannot ignore the possibility that Western Canadian nationalism could become more simply, and catastrophically, a nationalism for the West alone. In the face of chronic political alienation, could the region in whole or in part become so stressed that "the West wants in" becomes "the West wants *out*"?

THE FRAMEWORK OF ANALYSIS

In the exploration to come we will encounter a host of symbols and analogies that have been used by Western Canadians in an attempt to come to grips with their region, and with the relationship between the West and the broader Canadian community. Thus we will run into waves and surfers, melting pots, mosaics, and rednecks. All of these images reinforce our focus on perceptions and beliefs. What we want to outline is how Western Canadians see the political world, and part of that task is to uncover the symbols and stories that individuals use in trying to reduce a very complex political reality to more manageable terms. The appropriateness of those symbols and the veracity of the stories are less important than is their power to shape the political landscape.

The "West" to be addressed in this book is the land encompassed by the four provinces of Manitoba, Saskatchewan, Alberta, and British Columbia. This region covers 29 per cent of the Canadian landmass (48 per cent if we exclude the northern territories), and contains 29 per cent of the national population (see Figure 1.1).* We have not included the northern territories as part of the West, given their very different demography and physical environment. It should be noted, however, that Western Canadians frequently include the North within their perceptual map of the region, and therefore we may encounter some conceptual slippage throughout the analysis. The reader can assume that our use of "the West" does not include the Yukon and Northwest Territories, but should not assume that other people who are cited use the term in the same fashion. (W.A.C. Bennett, the former premier of British

FIGURE 1.1   Regional Distribution of the Canadian Population 1995

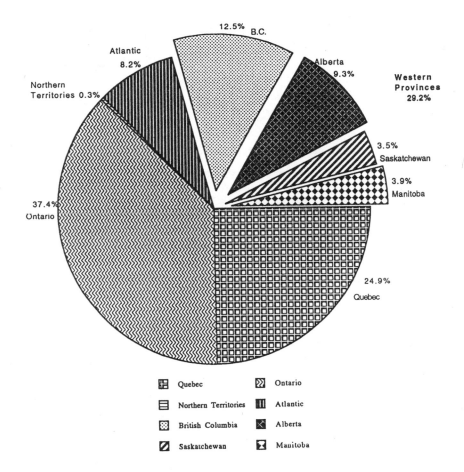

*Source*: Statistics Canada

The Population of Western Canada
1995

|  | Population | % of Regional Pop. |
|---|---|---|
| Manitoba | 1,132,800 | 13.2 |
| Saskatchewan | 1,017,200 | 11.8 |
| Alberta | 2,726,900 | 31.7 |
| British Columbia | 3,719,400 | 43.3 |
| The West | 8,596,300 | 100.0 |

Statistics Canada estimate for January 1, 1995.

Columbia, grafted the northern territories onto British Columbia and a new prairie province in his "five region" vision of Canada.) Considerable caution should also be exercised in folding Aboriginal peoples into the broader category "Western Canadians." Although Aboriginal peoples have placed an indelible stamp on the region, have contributed significantly to its political evolution, and will be major players in its future, their "national visions" are driven by quite different concerns and values than are those of the non-Aboriginal population. Thus any projection of broader regional sentiment onto Aboriginal peoples should be done with great care.

More generally, we are fully aware that the terms "Western Canadians," "Western Canada," and "the West" can mask and gloss over a good deal of heterogeneity within the region or, for that matter, within individual provinces. We will therefore be as alert to interprovincial and even intraprovincial differences as we can without losing our grip on regional themes, orientations, and visions. Survey data will be brought into play whenever possible to demonstrate regional homogeneity or heterogeneity, whichever may be the case. It should also be noted that phrases like "Western Canadians believe" should not be taken to imply that the beliefs at issue are necessarily idiosyncratic or unique to the region. In some cases what "the West thinks" may well parallel political beliefs and opinions elsewhere in the country. The western visions discussed herein are those which are important to the region, but such regional importance need not preclude the attractiveness of similar visions elsewhere in the country.

Throughout the analysis we will try to present the West through the words and writings of its residents. In many cases, this will mean a heavy reliance upon elected politicians for they, more than anyone else, have been central players in the attempt to articulate distinctive and coherent "western visions." Although the region's political elites have not always sung from the same hymn book, they have drawn from many of the same themes, symbols, and parables. However, we will also bring the perceptions, beliefs, and passions of those outside the formal political arena into play by drawing from comprehensive public opinion surveys.[2] At the same time, we make no claim to being systematic or representative in our sampling of Western Canadian political opinion. It is perhaps worth noting that we both come from the region, and are its products with respect to many of the predispositions and biases we bring to the study. This work is a synthesis and, in the final analysis, bears the stamp of these biases, as well as of our personalities. This has both strengths and weaknesses, and we can only hope that the former prevail.

A final caveat is that we have no pretensions about writing a comprehensive history of Western Canada, or even of painting a detailed picture of the region's political landscape. There is no dearth of good historical works on the Canadian West,[3] and no shortage of astute political commentary.[4] Our objective is more limited: it is to describe the evolution and contemporary nature of nationalist sentiment in Western Canada, and to offer some predictions as to how that sentiment might unfold in the years to come. We hope to place the West within the Canadian context, and to do so in a fashion that will be accessible to those who live within the region and to others who wish to strengthen their understanding of political life within the Canadian West. Indeed, the latter audience may be particularly important, for the "western visions" to be discussed have a relevance that reaches well beyond the region itself.

THE STORY TO COME

The next chapter examines the roots of the economic, social, and political discontent that has built up in the West since the early days of settlement. As we will show, a number of common themes have woven their way through the region's history, and these have been expressed by a vast array of political movements and actors. It should also become clear that there has been an explosive mix of fact and fiction: political perceptions have not been a simple reflection of the realities of the day (whatever they may be), but rather a reflection of those realities as seen by an often biased, even jaundiced, regional population. While we will certainly argue that there is substance to regional discontent about the place of the West within the broader national fabric, it is not our intention to provide a detailed empirical investigation of the realities of Confederation. We want to explore how Western Canadians *see* the world; the accuracy of those perceptions is a matter of secondary interest.

Chapter Three moves beyond the legacy of discontent to explore, in more positive terms, the "national visions" which Western Canadians have tried to articulate. As the chapter will illustrate, Western Canadians have advanced clear and emphatic visions of the kind of country Canada *should* be. However, while those visions are anchored in part to broader national values, they also run against the Canadian grain in some important respects. Political institutions and values which were more fully aligned with western visions would not be an easy sell in all parts of Canada.

Chapter Four examines the multitudinous political solutions that Western Canadians have proposed in the quest for a solution to regional grievances, and in the pursuit of their own national visions. We will examine how Western Canadians have used conventional party politics as a source of leverage on the national political system, and how they have also come up with a host of new parties and movements—the Progressives, Social Credit, the Cooperative Commonwealth Federation, and, most recently, the Reform Party of Canada. Similarly, we will examine the various reforms that have been proposed for national political institutions, how the West has challenged many of the basic conventions of Canadian political life, and how Western Canadians have tried to restructure both parliamentary democracy and federalism. The discussion will be brought to a close by a discussion of western separatism. Throughout, there is a common story to be told: while Western Canadians have sought a variety of structural and institutional reforms, they have encountered remarkably little success. They have not been able to impose western visions on Canada's institutional structures.

Explanations for this lack of success come in large part from the tensions that exist between those visions and ones that find their roots in Quebec, and more specifically in bicultural, binational conceptions of Canada. Chapter Five, therefore, explores the tensions that have existed and continue to exist between the West and Quebec. Although this exploration will focus to a degree on a series of specific disputes, the more fundamental tension comes from starkly conflicting national visions. The chapter will address the early roots of this tension in the patterns of agrarian settlement in Western Canada, and will then move forward in time to more contemporary manifestations.

The final chapter examines the future of the West. In so doing, we will be gazing into a very cloudy, even opaque crystal ball. As we write, Quebec stands poised for a provincial referendum on sovereignty. Until this referendum takes place and its results have been digested, all bets on the future of Canada, and on the future of the West, are off. Nonetheless, we will suggest in conclusion that the ties that bind the West to Canada are becoming frayed. It is therefore difficult to look ahead with any sense of unbridled optimism.

NOTES

1. Richard Allen, ed., *A Region of the Mind* (Regina: Canadian Plains Study Centre, University of Saskatchewan, 1973).
2. A number of surveys will be used extensively in the chapters to come. The 1992 Constitutional Referendum Survey was conducted in September and October, 1992, and included 2,530 respondents. It was part of the larger 1993 Canadian Election Study conducted by Richard Johnston, André Blais, Henry Brady, Elisabeth Gidengil, and Neil Nevitte. The "weighted" sample included 103 respondents from Manitoba, 92 from Saskatchewan, 231 from Alberta, and 315 from British Columbia. The Options for Western Canada Study was completed by the Angus Reid Group in May and June, 1991. It included 800 respondents

each from Alberta and British Columbia, 401 from Saskatchewan, and 403 from Manitoba. We will also draw from Gallup surveys, which normally have sample sizes of approximately 1,000 national respondents. This means that intraregional comparisons can seldom be made in the Gallup surveys.

3. For example, see Jean Barman, *The West Beyond the West* (Toronto: University of Toronto Press, 1991); Gerald Friesen, *The Canadian Prairies: A History* (Toronto: University of Toronto Press, 1984); James G. MacGregor, A History of Alberta, rev. ed. (Edmonton: Hurtig, 1981); David J. Mitchell, *W.A.C.: Bennett and the Rise of British Columbia* (Vancouver: Douglas & McIntyre, 1983); W.L. Morton, *The Progressive Party of Canada* (Toronto: University of Toronto Press, 1950) and *Manitoba: The Birth of a Province* (Altona: Friesen, 1965); Howard Palmer and Tamara J. Palmer, *Alberta, a New History* (Edmonton: Hurtig, 1990); and George Woodcock, *British Columbia: A History of the Province* (Vancouver: Douglas & McIntyre, 1990).

4. For examples, see Don Braid and Sydney Sharpe, *Breakup: Why the West Feels Left Out of Canada* (Toronto: Key Porter Books, 1990), and J.F. Conway, *The West: The History of a Region in Confederation*, second ed. (Toronto: James Lorimer, 1994). An excellent selection of readings is to be found in George Melnyk, ed., *Riel to Reform: A History of Protest in Western Canada* (Saskatoon: Fifth House Publishers, 1992).

# CHAPTER TWO

# The Roots of Regional Discontent

It is difficult to know where to begin a discussion of Western Canadian discontent. Part of the problem is that the sheer number and range of grievances can make the task encyclopedic. Then there is the problem that specific grievances are thoroughly entangled with one another, and have been woven into the broader tapestry of western alienation. Thus, for example, a discussion of economic complaints turns rapidly to the character of political parties, and then to the nature of parliamentary government. If regional discontent is not quite a seamless web, it is certainly one where the seams are hard to find and virtually impossible to pull apart. Moreover, grievances are so wrapped in legend and mythology that it is difficult to separate fact from fiction. We should also note the temporal span of western discontent. Not only are the roots of many contemporary issues to be found in the early decades of western settlement, but many grievances from the past continue to ripple through current debate; historical events are used as catalysts for present discontent. The slogan on Quebec licence plates—"je me souviens" or "I remember"—would be equally appropriate for the West, where residents have nurtured a long sense of historical grievance, and where even newcomers find it easy to adopt political rhetoric heavily laden with the sins of the past. Although Western Canadians may be forward looking as individuals, the regional political culture is often framed in terms of historical discontent.

Finally, when thinking about "western discontent" it is tempting and convenient to assume that the region is a single, cohesive entity. However, although it is often appropriate to note commonalities among the four western provinces, it is also important to remember the real and sometimes striking differences. As Nelson Wiseman suggests, treating the four as a single region "is akin to trying to tie four watermelons together with a single piece of string."[1] Variance in such matters as resources, economic activity, demography, political culture, continental location, and ideology serve to reinforce the jurisdictional boundaries among the provinces. (Saskatchewan is the only province or state in North America that has not adopted Daylight Saving Time!) As a consequence, there is no assurance that the region as a whole will rally around any specific point of grievance. As this chapter will show, the region can be drawn together analytically by a common set of themes, but the specific grievances used to illustrate those themes vary considerably from one province to the next. Although the story line may stay the same, the characters and the situations in which they find themselves change. We should begin, then, with a recognition of the diversity that exists within a region spanning more than a quarter of Canada's landmass.

REGIONAL HETEROGENEITY

As Figure 2.1 shows, the demographic composition of the West has changed dramatically over the past century. In the first two decades of the century a surge of immigration boosted Saskatchewan's population from 91,000 in 1901 to 758,000 in 1921, making it the largest of the four western provinces. With the onset of the Great Depression, however, Saskatchewan's population growth all but stopped: only 67,000 more people lived there at the time of the 1991 census than had lived in the province in 1931. The decade surrounding the Second World War marked a lasting change in the demographic composition of the West: Saskatchewan went from the largest western province in 1941 to the second smallest in 1951, and British Columbia became the largest. Manitoba's population continued to grow slowly throughout the century, but in relative terms it was quickly surpassed by both Alberta and British Columbia. In short, the region's demographic centre of gravity has moved steadily west, with over 43 per cent of the regional population now living in British Columbia. The two westernmost provinces combined contain 75 per cent of the Western Canadian population.

The dramatic demographic transformation charted in Figure 2.1 alerts us to a fluid and diverse regional environment. The most noticeable difference within the region is found between British Columbia and the three Prairie provinces. (Many British Columbians see their own province as "the West" and the other three simply as "the Prairies"; some describe British Columbia as "the coast" in contrast to the Prairies.) British Columbia entered Confederation under its own terms as a self-governing colony, whereas Alberta, Saskatchewan, and Manitoba were created by the federal government out of the Northwest Territories and, as such, experienced treatment bordering on colonialism. For example, while British Columbia had ownership of its resources from the time of entry into Confederation, the Prairie provinces did not gain ownership until 1930. When the three Prairie provinces were carved out of the former Northwest Territories, the ownership of natural resources and Crown land was retained by the federal government. Federal ownership, it can be argued, was essential if Ottawa was to be able to attract immigration and provide the infrastructure necessary for prairie settlement. Nonetheless, the fact that the Prairie provinces had a markedly different constitutional status from the other provinces rankled until the Natural Resources Transfer Act put the Prairie provinces on the same constitutional footing as the other

FIGURE 2.1　Provincial Composition of the Regional Population

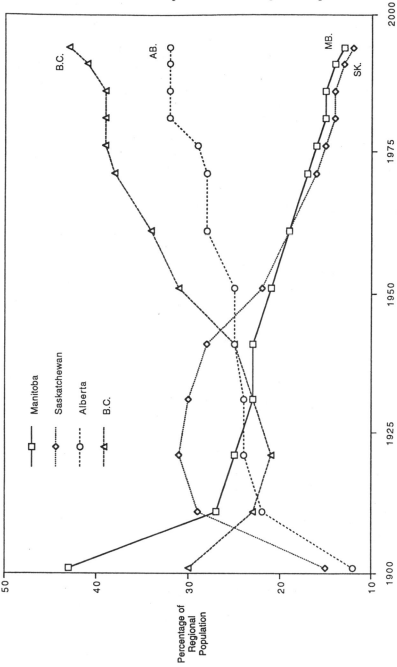

*Source*: Census Canada

provinces. This delay, and the associated struggle for provincial sovereignty with respect to natural resources, have had a particularly pronounced impact on the political culture of Alberta. The transfer of natural resources, however, is but one example in a broader pattern. Manitoba, for instance, owes its creation (in 1870) to the first rebellion of Louis Riel.[2] To Westerners more generally, the federal government seemed to step into Britain's shoes as the imperial government eased out of its colonial position. Exemplifying Ottawa's attitude was the fact that, of the 122 provincial statutes disallowed by the federal government between 1867 and 1946, 86 (70%) were from the four western provinces.[3]

British Columbia and the Prairie provinces are further distinguished from each other by the fact that they have been built upon quite different economic foundations. Whereas the economies of the Prairie provinces have depended heavily on the production of agricultural commodities and petroleum, the British Columbia economy has been based on forestry, pulp and paper, a wide range of minerals, and the fisheries. (Coal has also been important to the province's economy, and to that of Alberta.) This in turn creates different interests when it comes to national policies and world markets. While the British Columbia government concerns itself with balancing sustainable development with the demands of its forestry sector, the provincial governments in the Prairies are concerned with the world price of grain, and with international structures such as the Organization of Petroleum Exporting Countries (OPEC). The British Columbia economy is turned much more emphatically to the Pacific Rim than are the economies of the Prairie provinces. Furthermore, even within the Prairie provinces there is significant differentiation in the extent of economic reliance on agriculture and non-renewable natural resources. For instance, Alberta, with its bounty of petroleum resources, has a more diversified economy than that of the other two Prairie provinces. Moreover, the agricultural economy in Alberta is more diversified itself than are the wheat monocultures in Saskatchewan and Manitoba.

The distinction between British Columbia and "the rest" should not obscure a second important distinction, and that is between British Columbia and Alberta, on the one hand, and Saskatchewan and Manitoba, on the other. For at least the past fifty years, the two westernmost provinces have sustained much higher levels of economic prosperity and demographic growth. British Columbia and Alberta have been rivalled only by Ontario in terms of attractiveness for immigration and interprovincial migration, while the provincial populations of Saskatchewan and Manitoba have scarcely increased since the late 1920s. Prosperity has been a more fragile commodity in the eastern half of the region, and economic forecasts for the future are more subdued. It is therefore important to remember that the wealth commonly associated with Western Canada has not been evenly distributed across the region, and that disparities within the region often rival those between the West and other

Net Population Changes, 1992-93

When both immigration and interprovincial mobility are taken into account, Manitoba and Saskatchewan recorded net population losses between 1992 and 1993, whereas Alberta and particularly British Columbia posted net gains. The net gains and losses by province for 1992-93 were as follows:

|  | |  |
|---|---|---|
| Ontario | + | 107,655 |
| BC | + | 71,217 |
| Quebec | + | 32,747 |
| Alberta | + | 8,764 |
| Nova Scotia | + | 1,649 |
| PEI | + | 724 |
| New Brunswick | - | 1,477 |
| Manitoba | - | 2,394 |
| Newfoundland | - | 2,594 |
| Saskatchewan | - | 4,705 |

Ontario lost people through interprovincial migration, but attracted 121,844 immigrants. Proportionately, British Columbia was the fastest growing province: it gained 78,763 people from elsewhere in Canada, and lost 36,664 people to other provinces. Saskatchewan lost nearly 24,000 to other provinces while attracting 17,000 from other provinces and approximately 2,500 immigrants.

Source: Doug Fischer, "Canadians On Move Think West Best," *Calgary Herald*, August 5, 1994, p. A3.

regions of the country. One is reminded here of an often quoted difference between how things are done in Saskatchewan and Alberta. The Saskatchewan way is "great ideas and no money," whereas, at least in the eyes of Saskatchewan residents, the Alberta way is just the reverse.

With respect to recent economic performance, there are also significant differences between Saskatchewan and Manitoba. The period spanning the late 1980s and early 1990s was particularly grim for the relatively undiversified agricultural economy in Saskatchewan. More people moved out of the province than moved in, household incomes in 1991 were lower than they had been in 1980, and the number of operating farms fell by 2,600.[4] The province's desperate situation is illustrated by the opening lines in three successive reviews of Saskatchewan written for the *Canadian Annual Review* by J. R. Miller. The review for 1985 begins: "A dismal year for agriculture set the tone." In 1986, there is no improvement: "Economic problems made it a dismal year, and not even the diversions of an autumn election could lighten the mood." For 1987, Miller's bleak analysis continued: "It was a dismal and unproductive year, in both politics and the economy." This "dismal" state of the Saskatchewan economy was captured in the 1991 Angus Reid survey when respondents were asked about their level of satisfaction with the provincial economy. As Figure 2.2 shows, levels of satisfaction were dramatically lower in Saskatchewan than they were to the west or east. Although Manitoba respondents were not as satisfied as those in Alberta or British Columbia, their assessments were markedly more positive than those provided by Saskatchewan respondents.

Diversity within the West, and for that matter the distinctiveness of the region, is illustrated through reference to Aboriginal and environmental issues. With respect to the former, although it is clear that Aboriginal issues are at the centre of public policy disputes across the country, they take on particular importance in the West because of the relatively large size of the Aboriginal population and the added complexities of the issues. At the time of the 1991 census, 53 per cent of the Native population of Canada, and 60 per cent of the status Indian population, lived in the West. In Saskatchewan and Manitoba, or at least in significant parts of the two provinces, the Aboriginal population is increasing rapidly as a proportion of the total population.[5] For example, it has been estimated that within twenty years approximately thirty per cent of Saskatchewan's population could be of Aboriginal descent. The Prairie provinces also have a large Métis population and therefore, unlike other regions, the Métis play a significant role within Aboriginal and provincial politics. Alberta is the only province in which the Métis population, or at least the substantial part of that population living in Métis settlements, has a secure land base entrenched within the provincial constitution. In British Columbia, the lack of an established treaty framework has resulted in a large part of the province being claimed by First Nations, a feature that gives Aboriginal issues an edge that they may lack elsewhere in the region. Nowhere else, for example, is there a Native land claim with the magnitude and potential impact of the Nisga'a claim in northwestern British Columbia.

The environment is a second issue which, while clearly national and indeed global in character, plays out somewhat differently across the West. The most volatile cauldron of environmental politics at the present time is undoubtedly British Columbia, where disputes over the logging of old growth forests have sparked intense protest and have attracted widespread international attention. (Protests over logging in the Clayquot Sound area of Vancouver Island attracted such international luminaries as Robert Kennedy Jr. and the Australian rock band Midnight Oil.) Environmental politics are front and centre within the province to a degree unknown in the rest of the region, or in the rest of the country. As Vancouver Sun columnist Barbara Yaffe observes, "environmental protection is now the rage in B.C., with provincial politicians consistently embracing it over economic development."[6]

Given these differences within the region, and given quite different patterns

FIGURE 2.2    Satisfaction With Provincial Economy

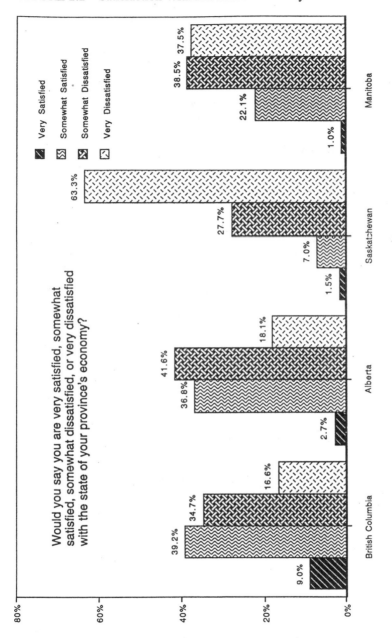

---

### Loggerheads Over Logs

In early 1995, a major dispute broke out between Alberta and British Columbia over the supply of logs to mills in the latter province. Logging restrictions in British Columbia forced mill operators in that province to purchase logs from private land owners and Indian reserves in Alberta. The resulting flow of logs from Alberta was so great that serious concerns were raised about environmental damage in Alberta. The Alberta environment minister, Ty Lund, blamed the environmental damage on the policies of the British Columbia government. The British Columbia forestry minister, Andrew Petter, called the charge "bizarre," and said that Alberta could learn a lot from British Columbia about forestry. Lund replied in turn by criticizing British Columbia's infringement of property rights, and said "Heaven forbid, we will never move to the socialist dictatorship that they're operating out there."

Source: Anthony Johnson, "Alberta, B.C. at Loggerheads Over Logs," *Calgary Herald*, February 25, 1995, A2.

---

of immigration across the four provinces, it is not surprising that the West has been characterized by a good deal of ideological diversity.[7] Alberta has traditionally been seen as the haven of right-wing conservatism, sometimes so much so that its inhabitants have been labelled "rednecks"—a derogatory term referring to those with a "lack of intellect, culture and tolerance."[8] However, as the *Globe and Mail* reports, the term is in the midst of being redefined and even lauded in some parts of the province where people are "frustrated by the pervasiveness of political correctness, the erosion of traditional family values and the prospect of yet another constitutional showdown centering on Quebec."[9] In short, the new Albertan meaning for "redneck" is someone who wants to put "common sense back into the system."[10] It is interesting in this context to note a comment by Vancouver Sun columnist Gordon Gibson, who was observing how long it takes "the central Canadian media" to discover political truths "known in Outer Canada for a generation." As Gibson points out, the redneck views of Western Canadians get transformed in the process: "Ah well, I guess that ideas that turn necks a bright red out here just get bleached into a nice healthy pink when they flow from the authorized pens and mouths of the Liberals-and-points-left media back East."[11]

Although the term "redneck" has been connected most closely with Alberta, it has been used at times to describe those living farther to the east. However, the ideological climate in Saskatchewan has been much more receptive to left-of-centre parties than has been the case in Alberta.[12] The CCF, although founded at a meeting in Calgary in 1932, enjoyed its greatest success in Saskatchewan, where the NDP has been the dominant provincial party in

recent decades. The NDP has also enjoyed greater success in Manitoba, where it placed a strong second in the 1995 provincial election, than it has in Alberta. There has been, then, considerable ideological diversity across the Prairies, just as there have undoubtedly been some important ideological differences between the western and central Canadian wings of national parties. For example, NDP provincial governments led by Ontario's Bob Rae and Saskatchewan's Roy Romanow have been far from identical in their approach to social program reform and deficit reduction; Saskatchewan brought in a balanced budget in 1995 whereas Ontario's anticipated provincial deficit that

---

Manitoba and Doughnuts

In a column published in the *Globe and Mail*, Vancouver columnist Robert Mason Lee accused federal cultural institutions of creating a "doughnut nation." The hole at the centre is Manitoba, a hole which CBC and Newsworld try to fill every four years during the provincial election campaign, and then ignore. As Lee concludes, "in the doughnut nation of the future [Manitoba] will rise every four years on election day, then fade again into the mist, like Brigadoon." Winnipeg writer and historian Allan Levine then expanded this analogy by referring to Manitoba as the "Timbit" of the nation. Levine, however, was less troubled by the lack of media attention received by Manitoba. "In the final analysis, it doesn't matter to most Manitobans whether the rest of the country knows the province exists. In fact, better that Mr. Lee and other journalists continue preserving our privacy; otherwise, who knows who will want to move here and ruin it for the rest of us."

Robert Mason Lee, "Have the Feds Created a Doughnut Nation?" *Globe and Mail*, April 1, 1995, p. D2.

Allan Levine, "Manitoba: The `Timbit' of the Nation," *Globe and Mail*, April 4, 1995, p. A21.

---

year surpassed California's, despite the fact that the latter's population is almost three times that of the former.[13]

Of the four western provinces, British Columbia is the most isolated and undoubtedly most distinct member of the regional community. As George Woodcock explains in the introduction to his history of the province, ". . . I have been able to see British Columbia as a land in its special right, a place and a culture whose changing patterns have their own life, for the province has belonged only relatively briefly and never completely to the larger political entities in which it has been involved."[14] Joe Clark's perceptions, although formed at a greater distance, parallel those of Woodcock:

> ... psychologically, I think that British Columbia is the province most separated from the rest of Canada ... there is not much interest in the larger country, not much sense of connection or of relevance. That stark ridge of Rocky Mountains is much more than a symbolic barrier. It is a line of real demarcation.[15]

Yet the province's political life is far from being disconnected from national ideological currents; debates within the province may take on a different tone and amplitude than they do elsewhere, but they are recognizable nonetheless. British Columbia presents one of the most complex and polarized ideological environments in the country and, perhaps not coincidentally, it is also the most unionized environment. The traditionally dominant parties in the province sing from completely different ideological hymn books. The conservative Social Credit party (now virtually extinct) and the left-of-centre CCF/NDP were locked in battle for generations, and offered voters radically different ideological visions. (As is often the case, the two parties differed less in government than they did on the campaign trail.) The current ideological stew has been made more complex by a resurgent if somewhat unstable Liberal party, and by the vigorous entry of the Reform party into provincial politics. (The BC Reform party has no official connection to the Reform Party of Canada, but the two draw from overlapping constituencies and ideological convictions.) Whether these new political players will moderate or exacerbate ideological polarization within the province remains to be seen.

In drawing this overview to a close, we should note that variation within the West finds reflection in the current political agendas of the four provinces. Manitoba and Saskatchewan wrestle with low levels of economic and population growth, a beleaguered agricultural economy, and the growing assertiveness of Aboriginal communities. In this last respect, Manitoba is also the site of dramatic self-government initiatives by the federal Department of Indian Affairs, whereby a 1994 framework agreement will soon enable 60 First Nations to assume most responsibilities currently exercised by the department. Alberta is transfixed by the politics of debt and deficit reduction, downsizing, and privatization. Although these issues have not been ignored elsewhere in the region, they have not driven all other issues off the political stage to the same extent as they have in Alberta, where the Social Credit's monetary legacy, the sudden fall from financial grace that accompanied the collapse of world oil prices in the early 1980s, and a string of disastrous economic diversification gambles by the provincial government have given "deficit politics" a particularly hard edge. British Columbia is faced with complex environmental and Aboriginal issues that are far more central to the political agenda than they are elsewhere in the West. We must therefore be careful when making broad regional generalizations. Caution, however, does not preclude an attempt to come to grips with regional patterns and trends.

ECONOMIC DISCONTENT

The stereotypical view of Western Canadian discontent is that it all boils down to dollars and cents, that the basic problem lies with the place of the West in the national and continental economies. This view is contested within the region, at least to a degree, for a number of reasons. First, Western Canadians suspect that such a view erodes the legitimacy or priority of regional discontent; the protection of economic interests is portrayed as less important than the defence of cultural interests, and Western Canadians are thus depicted as fighting on the low ground of money rather than on the high ground of culture. Second, this view discounts or ignores the positive national visions that

Western Canadians have tried so hard to promote, visions discussed at length in the next chapter. And third, those outside the region often fail to appreciate that economic discontent is, at heart, political discontent: Western Canadians believe that most of the economic problems they have faced in the past and face today are rooted in the nature and bias of political institutions.

Nonetheless, there is an important element of truth in the stereotype: economic grievances are not the sum total of regional discontent, but they do lie at the core of that discontent. Simply put, Western Canadians believe that the national economy has been rigged to their disadvantage, and to the advantage of the Central Canadian provinces and their economic interests. As a consequence, it is believed that Western Canadians have not received a fair return on their contribution to the national economy; their aspirations have not been fully realized within an economic order that is seen to be exploitative, almost colonial in character. Although this belief may have weakened in the wake of the Free Trade Agreement and its creation of a more fully integrated continental economy, and may weaken further in the wake of NAFTA and economic globalization, it is still the core belief in the syndrome of western alienation.

But what evidence do Western Canadians bring into play in making and sustaining this argument? As we suggested in the introduction to this chapter, there is a multitude of economic grievances from which to draw. The following have been selected for their relatively high profile, and because they illustrate more general themes of regional discontent.

*The National Policy*

Introduced in 1879, the National Policy was designed to encourage the industrialization of Canada through the construction of a tariff wall between Canada and the United States. (Tariffs would also help finance the railway construction upon which western settlement depended.) The expectation was that American firms would jump the tariff wall by setting up branch plants north of the border, creating Canadian jobs as they did so. However, while the costs of higher priced imports were to be carried by all Canadians, the benefits of industrialization seemed to accrue almost entirely to the Central Canadian provinces. When, over the following decades, firms jumped the wall, they tended to land in Montreal and Toronto rather than in Winnipeg, Saskatoon, Calgary, or Vancouver. In this sense, tariffs were seen to work to the disadvantage of Westerners who paid their share of the tariff cost but reaped none of the benefits. Moreover, western agricultural producers found themselves at a considerable disadvantage in competing against American farmers on world markets. The Canadians faced higher input costs because of the tariff, but received the same international price for their product as American farmers received.[16]

*Freight rates*

National freight rates were set historically by the federal government to reflect the highly competitive transportation network in Central Canada, and the lack of any viable alternative to rail transportation in Western Canada. As a consequence, freight rates were relatively low in the east and high in the west. Furthermore, it was often the case that it cost more to move goods out of Western Canada than to move goods in. More specifically, and more problematically, it was cheaper to ship out unprocessed, raw resources from the West than it was to ship out processed material, hence creating a disincentive for locating manufacturing operations in the West. Thus, when the freight rate structure was viewed from a regional perspective, western producers and consumers were seen to be subsidizing Central Canadian manufacturers. Saskatchewan premier Allan Blakeney's 1977 presentation to the Task Force on Canadian Unity nicely captures the regional perspective:

> In Saskatchewan we have grown accustomed to the assumption by Ontario and Quebec that they constitute Canada. It does not surprise us to discover participants in the current debate defending Canada entirely from the perspective of Central Canada. Most currently-available histories of Canada, after all, adopt the same view. For them the last spike serves to bind the West to the great metropolitan centres of Central Canada; for us, it is a constant reminder of discriminatory freight rates and land grants to the CPR ...[17]

It should be noted, incidentally, that freight rates were a far greater concern on the Prairies than they were in British Columbia, where relatively inexpensive water transportation kept rail rates low, and where there was no need to move grain thousands of kilometres to world markets. Related concerns on the Prairies addressed bottlenecks in the transportation of prairie grain to ocean ports and, at least prior to the creation of the Canadian Wheat Board, the excessive profits of middlemen in the grain trade.

The lightning rod for regional discontent with freight rates and transportation policy has always been the Crow rate, established by the Crow's Nest Pass Agreement in 1897. The Crow rate eventually provided a massive public subsidy for the shipment of unprocessed prairie grain, and it was staunchly defended by grain producers. However, it came under increased pressure from American farmers, from international reductions in agricultural subsidies, and from those promoting a more diversified agricultural economy in Western Canada, while the Saskatchewan government remained its most ardent defender. In 1982, for example, then attorney general Roy Romanow declared that "abolishing the Crow rate is an attempt by the federal government to break the Confederation bargain at the expense of the Western farmer."[18] In 1995, Premier Romanow grimly predicted that the abolition of the Crow and related subsidies under the Western Grain Transportation Act would lead to the massive restructuring of rural Saskatchewan.[19] In the end, however, Saskatchewan's protests were in vain; subsidies ended on August 1, 1995, and farmers were left to divide up nearly $1.6 billion in compensation.

## The National Energy Program

The NEP was introduced in 1980 in response to a dramatic increase in the world price of oil. It was designed to encourage the Canadianization of the oil industry, to shift exploration from proven fields in the provinces to federal Crown land in the North, and to redistribute revenues among the producers, the provinces involved, and the federal government. It was also designed to protect Canadian consumers, most of whom lived outside the producing provinces, by imposing a limit on the price of oil. The NEP is widely believed, particularly in Alberta, to have had a devastating impact on the health of the industry and the Canadian economy more generally. The Alberta government estimates that the province lost at least $50 billion in tax revenue as a direct consequence of the NEP, and although the impact of the NEP was greatest in Alberta, the premiers of both Manitoba and Saskatchewan supported Alberta's opposition. The fact that Alberta lacked elected representation in the federal Liberal government which created the NEP was not seen as coincidental.

## Federal spending patterns

The West as a whole, and Alberta and British Columbia in particular, have been net contributors to regional economic development and equalization programs; western taxpayers have put more into these programs than the region has received in return. By itself, this "inequity" has not been a major source of discontent although, as we will see in the next chapter, British Columbia has expressed reservations about equalization payments. However, when combined with the perception that Ottawa's discretionary spending also works to the disadvantage of the region, it becomes a source of discontent. Western Canadians believe, with considerable empirical justification, that federal spending on such things as research and development, supplies and services, and cultural activities is systematically biased to the advantage of Central Canada.

The most global evidence for this conviction, although it also illustrates differences within the West, comes from a study published in 1995 by economists Robert Mansell and Ronald Schlenker.[20] The authors examined federal government spending from 1961 to 1992, and found that $46 billion less had been spent in the region than had been taken out through federal taxes. However, on a provincial basis only Alberta was a net loser; its loss of $138.8 billion compared to gains of $6.1, $36.4 and $50.3 billion in British Columbia, Saskatchewan, and Manitoba respectively. Quebec's gain during

Perceived Bias of the Federal Government

In a late 1993 survey conducted by Decima Research for *Maclean's/* CTV, 1610 respondents were asked if they thought the newly elected Liberal government would favour any region or province over another. Respondents from the West were much more likely to anticipate favouritism, and in most cases identified Quebec as the favoured province.

|  | *% saying yes* | *% saying new federal govt. would favour Quebec* |
|---|---|---|
| BC | 50 | 46 |
| Alberta | 50 | 42 |
| Saskatchewan | 39 | 38 |
| Manitoba | 41 | 28 |
| Ontario | 26 | 22 |
| Quebec | 27 | 7 |
| New Brunswick | 27 | 16 |
| Nova Scotia | 30 | 19 |
| PEI | 29 | 17 |
| Newfoundland | 19 | 18 |

Source: *Maclean's*, January 3, 1994, p. 16.

the same period was $167.6 billion, compared to an Ontario loss of $45 billion.

Perhaps the most politically charged confirmation of this belief in recent memory came from the federal government's 1986 decision to award the CF-18 maintenance contract to Canadair in Montreal despite an internal departmental review which showed that the bid from the Bristol group, based in Winnipeg, was superior on financial and technical grounds.[21] The decision was a pivotal event in the launching of the Reform party,[22] and it has played a role in Manitoba politics analogous to that played by the NEP in Alberta. Geoffrey Lambert argues that the CF-18 decision, which was seen to deny Manitoba's rightful place in the technological sun, had a profound effect on political sentiment in the province:

The substance of the decision naturally distressed Manitobans, since the national government set aside normal tendering procedures in preference to political calculations. Once again, many felt, cynical political considerations had favoured central Canada at the expense of the west. The anger in Manitoba was the greater because Bristol's bid (all parties acknowledged) was cheaper and had been judged technically superior by a panel of federal government experts.[23]

*Debt and deficit*

Governments across Canada, and at all levels, face a serious problem with respect to deficits and the accumulated debt. These are issues with great historical resonance in Western Canada; they provided much of the fodder for Alberta's Social Credit movement and were identified in the founding document of the CCF as one of the primary problems to be addressed. The 1933 Regina Manifesto stated:

> An inevitable effect of the capitalist system is the debt creating character of public financing. All public debts have enormously increased, and the fixed interest charges paid thereon now amount to the largest single item of so-called uncontrollable public expenditures. The C.C.F. proposes that in future no public financing shall be permitted which facilitates the perpetuation of the parasitic interest-receiving class....

In recent years, the western provinces have made substantial progress in reducing their operating deficits, and all four predicted balanced or surplus budgets for the 1995-96 fiscal year. (Saskatchewan was the first to bring down a balanced budget in 1995.) At the same time, the deficit situation in Ontario and Quebec, and for the federal government, is dramatically different. Optimistic projections for Ottawa still forecast a deficit of $18 to $20 billion by 1997-98, and there is little sign that the huge provincial deficits in Ontario and Quebec are about to be slashed, much less eliminated. Hence the increased likelihood, indeed almost certainty, that debt and deficit issues will come to be seen in *regional* terms. The deficit-free West will be portrayed as struggling under the cross of a national deficit sustained by a profligate federal government.

\* \* \* \* \* \*

If we look beyond the details of these specific issues, we find an important pattern. Virtually all can be traced to actions taken by the federal government: *Ottawa* built the tariff wall, fixed the freight rates, established the National Energy Program, and spent the country into the ground. To borrow from the feminist slogan, "the personal is political," the conclusion in the West is that "the economic is political." Somehow a line seemed to be drawn between the *Canadian* economy (a.k.a. the *Central Canadian* economy) and the *regional* economy, a line that enabled the federal government to sacrifice the interests of the latter for the interests of the former. As Ted Byfield has observed, "the National Interest curiously always corresponds with the Toronto interest."[24] In this respect, Joe Clark identifies the core of western alienation as "the conviction that, when the `Canadian national interest' is defined, the West is not taken seriously."[25]

The bottom line for Western Canadians was nicely captured by two questions asked in the 1991 Western Canada Study conducted by Angus Reid. Respondents were asked: "On balance, would you say that the West has gained or lost economically as a result of being part of Canada?" Overall, 50.7 per cent felt that the West had lost, compared to 35 per cent who felt the West had gained. Interestingly, there were no significant inter-provincial differences; the percentage saying that on balance the West had lost ranged only from 47.4 per cent in Manitoba to 52.3 per cent in British Columbia. Respondents were also asked the following question: "Over the past few years, do you think the policies of the federal government have helped your province's economy, hurt your province's economy, or have not made much difference to the overall health of your province's economy?" Across the region, 58.8 per cent said the federal government had hurt their province's economy, 33 per cent could detect no difference, and only 5.8 per cent said that the federal government had helped. In this case, however, there were quite sharp provincial differences within which can be detected echoes of the CF 18 affair. The percentage of respondents who said that the federal government had hurt their provincial economy ranged from a high of 76.9 per cent in Manitoba to 58.2 per cent in Alberta, 54.6 per cent in British Columbia, and 50.1 per cent in Saskatchewan.

All of the above is not to say that Western Canadians have been blind to very real disadvantages their region faces within the national, continental, and world economies. The western provinces lie at the periphery of the continental economy, and lack the population base to sustain a strong manufacturing base. (The marginalization of the West is more of a concern for the Prairie provinces than it is for British Columbia; while the latter may be on the periphery of the continental economy, it provides the continental gateway to the booming economies of the Pacific Rim.) It is unlikely, for example, that major industries would have been established in Regina or Lethbridge no matter what the nature of the national tariff policy had been, for they were simply too remote from continental and international markets.[26] Nor have Western Canadians been blind to the problems inherent in selling natural resources on an unstable and volatile international market. They realize, for example, that no amount of federal assistance could have totally ironed out the booms and busts as regional producers of coal, natural gas, oil, potash, timber, and wheat struggled for some security within the international market. When the demand for Western Canadian products has been strong and prices high, the region has prospered; when demand has faltered and prices have fallen, the region has suffered. Nonetheless, the core complaint remains. To the extent that the federal government has intervened in the economic order, it is perceived to have done so to the detriment and not to the advantage of the West. The reality of this complaint is beside the point; it is etched indelibly on the regional political culture.

It should be noted here that conflict between the West and the Central

Perceptions Vary

Our focus throughout this chapter is on how Western Canadians *see* the economic and political worlds. However, the veracity of those perceptions is open
to legitimate debate. As in most matters, where one stands depends on where
one sits. Note the very different perception of University of Toronto historian J.
M. S. Careless:

> ... it is still true that the West as we now know it came into being only under a cen-
> tral, national design—and this included building east-west trade behind a tariff
> wall. How could the designers think otherwise than in terms of centrally directed
> purposes, when a western regional society had yet to be created? The imposition
> of the tariff was not just centralist greed and self-interest, but part of a genuine
> nation-making effort. The achievement of this design, in fact, was the rapid set-
> tling of the West, which then increasingly protested central domination - and the
> policy which had helped make the modern West possible.

Source: J. M. S. Careless, "The Myth of the Downtrodden West," in Mark
Charlton and Paul Barker (eds.), *Contemporary Political Issues* (Toronto:
Nelson Canada, 1994), p. 53.

Canadian provinces, or between the western provincial governments and the
federal government, has not been restricted to economic issues. There have
been serious disagreements with respect to national policies on such things as
bilingualism, environmental protection, immigration, and extra billing in the
health care field. In 1995, the federal government's gun control legislation
opened up another regional cleavage as the three Prairie provincial governments, along with those of the northern territories, strongly opposed a measure described by Saskatchewan New Democratic MP Chris Axworth as a
"prairie lifestyle tax."[27] (*Maclean's* business columnist Peter C. Newman
went so far as to describe the gun control legislation as the "CF-18 of the
1990s."[28]) However, these conflicts would not be sufficient to strain the
national fabric were it not also for the economic grievances and underlying
dissatisfaction regarding western input into national decision-making.

Although Western Canadians largely share the perception that the West has
fared badly within Confederation, the region has been marked more by its relative prosperity than by economic hardship. Admittedly, the situation in
Manitoba and particularly Saskatchewan has been precarious in recent years,
but the region as a whole has prospered, with Alberta and British Columbia
generally registering rates of economic growth and personal income significantly above the national average. However, the relationship between prosperity and political discontent has been the reverse of what we might expect;
Western discontent has often peaked during times of strong economic perfor-

mance and relative wealth. For example, political discontent in Alberta came to a boil in the early 1980s when escalating oil prices were bestowing unprecedented wealth on the province and its residents. Taxes were low, public spending was nothing short of lavish, and the provincial government was still able to salt away more than $12 billion in the Alberta Heritage Savings and Trust Fund. Protest was not sparked by depression or poverty, but by the perception of Albertans that they were being denied the full fruits of their natural resource endowment. It was the $50 billion that the province supposedly lost as a consequence of the National Energy Program that sparked the outrage; the province's relative and absolute prosperity was irrelevant.

It is not unusual, incidentally, for there to be a stronger association between economic prosperity and political discontent than between poverty and discontent. As Ted Gurr has shown in a broad international survey of political discontent,[29] the most volatile times politically are often those in which sustained periods of economic prosperity are followed by a sudden downturn in the economy. Periods of sustained poverty, or for that matter sustained prosperity, are less likely to spark revolt. As Gurr has shown, it is relative rather than absolute poverty that generates discontent. In the case of the contemporary West, the critical comparison has been with the wealth the region *might* have enjoyed were it not for the intervention of the federal government. However, the fact also remains that the West's combination of prosperity and political discontent has not played well outside the region, where such discontent has often been seen as unreasonable whining by the country's most privileged region. In short, it has been difficult for Western Canadians to find a sympathetic audience, just as it has been difficult for Quebec nationalists to convince English Canadians that Quebec has suffered at the hands of the federal government. As both Western Canadians and Quebec nationalists have found out, plays that draw enthusiastic audiences at home may bomb when taken on the road.

POLITICAL DISCONTENT

Some of the economic problems that Western Canadians have faced, or have perceived, may well have come about without political intervention. For example, the harsh reaction of Central Canadian banks to the desperate plight of prairie farmers during the Great Depression may have had more to do with the nature of banks than with the nature of politics. However, tariffs, freight rates, and policies such as the National Energy Program were political artifacts. What needs to be explained, then, is how the political system has worked to the systematic disadvantage of Western Canadian interests. Here there is no shortage of explanations, all of which confirm W.L. Morton's early thesis that "the initial bias of prairie politics was the fact of political subordination in Confederation."[30]

The various protest movements and parties in Western Canada have expressed a common belief that the political rules of the game are fixed in favour of a broadly defined Central Canada, and more specifically in favour of the economic elites located in the east. (The belief that Quebec *per se* is the prime beneficiary is of relatively recent vintage.[31]) There is a perceived linkage between the litany of economic problems confronting Western Canadians—bottlenecks in the movement of grain, excessive freight rates, high tariffs on agricultural equipment, exploitative interest rates, insensitive financial institutions—and the nature of the political system. The sinews of that linkage are provided by party discipline in the House of Commons, which makes it difficult for Western MPs to defend regional interests, and by party and electoral systems which lodge political power in the heavily populated Central Canadian provinces. Although this argument has become somewhat more complex in recent years, its basic features have been staples of western alienation for generations.

There is a relatively straightforward story line to political discontent in the West, and it begins with the role of Western MPs in Ottawa. It is a long-standing belief that MPs are not responsive to their regional constituents, that upon arriving on Parliament Hill they become beholden to a set of partisan and financial interests which work systematically to the disadvantage of the West. In the early part of this century, this belief stemmed in part from the geographical isolation of the region; Western MPs really were cut off from their constituents during sessions of Parliament, and there was an understandable feeling among constituents that their MPs came to see the world from the perspective of Ottawa rather than the West. This perception persists today, although it may have abated somewhat in the face of vastly improved transportation and communication technologies. As Figure 2.3 shows, only 28 per cent of respondents in the 1991 Angus Reid poll felt that their MP was doing a good or very good job. (The provincial figures ranged from a low of 22.5% in Alberta to a high of 32.3% in British Columbia.) However, if western MPs are still cut off, the problem is only partially one of distance, although distance remains a serious problem for British Columbia MPs, given that Vancouver is three time zones and five hours by air from Ottawa, with MPs from the province's interior being at an even greater disadvantage. The more basic problem is the party discipline to which MPs are tied. Indeed, party discipline is *the* problem in the mythology of Western Canadian political discontent, even though party discipline is not seen to be a problem within *provincial* legislatures. In the final analysis, it is believed, Western MPs must toe the party line, and if this means that regional interests and the local interests of constituents are sacrificed to the larger interests of party, then so be it.

Party discipline finds its roots in the basic principles of responsible, parliamentary democracy. The government of the day is "responsible" to the House of Commons because it must resign if it fails to command majority support. Therefore government MPs naturally rally behind the government to prevent defeat on the floor of the House.[32] Thus the tenets of responsible gov-

FIGURE 2.3   Effectiveness of Federal MPs

"Generally speaking, would you say your federal Member of Parliament is doing a very good, good, fair, poor, or very poor job of representing your community's interests in Ottawa?"

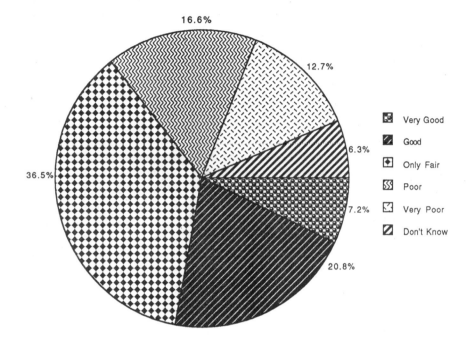

*Source*: Angus Reid, Options for Western Canada, 1991 Survey   N = 2406

ernment, the fact that the cabinet must retain majority support in the House, and the lack of fixed election dates, all make party discipline an integral part of Canadian parliamentary democracy. It is important to note, however, that the constraints of party discipline are tighter in Canada than they are in other parliamentary democracies, including the United Kingdom, and that party discipline has come to dominate the general ethos and normative structure of the House of Commons. In other words, party discipline is the name of the parliamentary game even when the fate of the government is not on the line. We find this, for example, in the daily Question Period, where partisanship shapes the entire tenor and tone of debate. Straight questions, which are rarely asked, rarely receive straight answers.

But why is party discipline a particular problem for the West? It is, after all, a constraint faced by MPs from all regions of the country. The problem arises because of the *combination* of party discipline with the regional distribution of the Canadian population. The western spin comes from the belief that the national political parties are particularly beholden to vote-rich Ontario and Quebec electorates, and—albeit less directly—to the financial and commercial interests located within those provinces. *Therefore the interests of party become the interests of Central Canada.* Put more bluntly, the perception is that the Western MP who puts his or her party ahead of regional interests is in effect putting the interests of the Central Canadian electorate ahead of regional interests, whereas an MP from Ontario or Quebec who sacrifices region to party is not making any sacrifice at all. While Western MPs may lobby vigorously on behalf of regional interests in private, behind the closed doors of cabinet and party caucuses, their *public* behaviour is heavily constrained by party discipline. Hence the impression that Western MPs have sold out.

The problem, then, only begins with party discipline. It expands when one takes into account that 62 per cent of the Canadian population resides in Ontario and Quebec,[33] and that the country's major financial interests and political capital region are lodged within those provinces. In the early decades of this century, there was particular concern about the impact of the banks and related corporate interests, such as the Canadian Pacific Railway, on Western interests. Note, for example, the following passage from *The Case for Alberta*, prepared in 1938 by the government of Alberta for the Royal Commission on Dominion-Provincial Relations:

> The heavy price which Alberta and other western provinces have paid for their membership in Confederation has created a growing resentment towards the east in the minds of westerners. This threatens to strike at the very roots of national unity. Yet the people of the east are not to blame for the plight of the west, for they are also the victims of the same interests which have reduced the western provinces to a condition of economic impotence. Until this is recognized, and until the people of the east join hands with the people of the west to

overcome the forces of reaction supporting the dominating financial interests, there will be little hope of a United Canada so essential to Confederation....[34]

Perhaps all that has changed today is that Western Canadians are no longer inclined to let "the people of the east" off the hook. The contemporary emphasis is much more on the political weight of the Central Canadian electorate, and less on financial interests.

The basic complaint, therefore, has been that Western Canadians are entangled in a political system that does not permit the fair and effective representation of regional interests. MPs are constrained by party discipline, and party interests tend to boil down to Central Canadian interests. Western MPs might lobby privately for regional interests, but they cannot do so in a visible or transparent manner. Senators, appointed as they are by the federal government, are seen as retired party warhorses or fundraisers whose interests start and stop with their party, a characterization which may be harsh but which is not far off the mark. Western representatives are to be found in Ottawa, but effective representation is not.

This critique, which is by no means unique to the West, extends to cabinet, the institutional heart of Canadian parliamentary government. Given the cabinet's dominance over both the legislative and administrative branches of government, it is not surprising that the cabinet is the most important *representative* institution in Canada. Inclusion within the cabinet is the litmus test for any group or region's importance in the political scheme of things. The western critique, however, has not focused on the cabinet's failure to include Western representatives, for this has seldom happened. (It was a problem during the Liberals' national dominance from 1972 to 1984, a period when Liberal MPs were scarce in the West and unknown in Alberta, and when regional representation in cabinet was largely entrusted to Liberal senators.) Rather, the critique has addressed the *nature* of cabinet representation. The conventions of collective responsibility and secrecy mean that cabinet speaks with a single voice. As a consequence, the regional representation and advocacy that may be taking place within cabinet are invisible to voters, and there is no evidence of effective representation. It should not be surprising, then, that Figure 2.4 shows such a negative regional assessment of the effectiveness of regional representation in cabinet. If the cabinet comes up with a policy that appears to run counter to regional interests, ministers have no option but to defend that policy in public. Voters are therefore left with unanswered and unanswerable questions. Were "their" ministers out-muscled in cabinet? Did they fight the good fight but lose? Did their protestations result in a policy that was not as bad as it could have been? Were trade-offs reached on other policies which were more favourable to the region? Or were their ministers asleep at the switch? Did they sell out their region for the larger interests of party or "national unity"?

The fact that these questions cannot be answered has meant that Western

Canadians have turned to their provincial premiers to articulate and defend regional interests. Premiers may not be more effective than regional representatives within cabinet, but their voice is unconstrained by secrecy, collective responsibility, or party discipline. In the absence of an elected Senate and in the presence of a House tightly bound by the constraints of party discipline, the premiers emerge as the most strident and visible regional representatives. As a consequence, executive federalism and First Ministers' Conferences often appear to eclipse Parliament as the principal regional arena. In the 1991 Angus Reid survey, 50.5 per cent of the regional respondents approved of their provincial government's track record in representing provincial interests in Ottawa, whereas 40.1 per cent disapproved.

The thesis that parliamentary institutions are inherently biased against Western Canadian interests was put to a critically important test following the 1984 federal election. During the years from 1972 to 1984, when the Liberals were in power in Ottawa,[35] the West was all but shut out of the governing Liberal caucus and cabinet as the region continued to support the Conservative party. (In the 1972, 1974, and 1980 elections combined, the four western provinces elected only 22 Liberal MPs, compared to 140 PC and 51 New Democratic MPs.) The nadir came in 1980, when only two Western Liberal MPs, both from Manitoba, were elected. In such circumstances, it was difficult to separate institutional bias from the effects of partisanship. Hence the question: might parliamentary institutions provide effective representation if the right party, or the right leader, were in office? Did the West simply need a change in government rather than a change in the nature of parliamentary government? The opportunity to answer this question came in 1984, when Brian Mulroney's Progressive Conservatives swept into power. Western MPs were suddenly at the centre of power, and thus Westerners had the chance to see if better representation within cabinet[36] and the governing caucus would provide better representation for the West within Canada.

And to an extent, the situation did improve for the West. The National Energy Program was dismantled, albeit tardily, and the Western Energy Accord was put in its place. Substantial financial relief was provided to prairie farmers facing drought and depressed world grain prices. In Mulroney's second term, the Western Diversification Office (WDO) was established, and in fiscal 1988-89 the WDO was awarded $312 million to promote new economic activity in the region. The prime minister turned out to be a passionate supporter of free trade, a cause long supported on the Prairies (see Chapter Four). Yet despite all this, western alienation remained strong, and reinforced a growing antipathy to the Mulroney government shared by Canadians from coast to coast. The Conservatives' share of the Western Canadian vote dropped from 51.9 per cent in the 1984 general election to 40.4 per cent in 1988, a decline of 11.5 per cent compared to a decline of only 5.4 per cent outside the West. Whether it was the legacy of the CF-18 decision, the early emergence of Reform, the plummeting agricultural economy in Sas-

FIGURE 2.4   Effectiveness of Cabinet Representation

"There are more Ministers for the West in the Federal Cabinet today than at any other time in recent history. Some people say this means that the interests of Western Canadians are well represented in decisions made by the Federal Government. Others say that, even though there are more Western Ministers, Western Canadian concerns really aren't well represented in the decisions made by the Federal Government. Generally speaking, which viewpoint is closest to yours?"

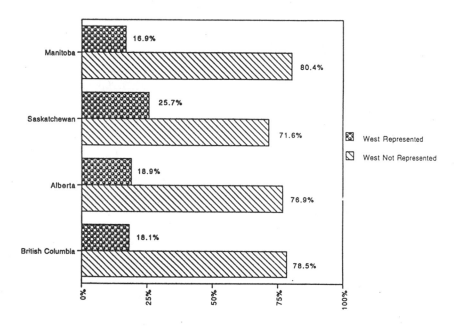

*Source*: Options for Western Canada Study 1991

katchewan, or the prime minister's constitutional preoccupation with Quebec—the cause is difficult to determine, but the outcome remains the same. Fairly or not, Westerners came to the conclusion that it did not matter which party was in office. Thus, the West was faced with the challenge of finding a new strategy to achieve equality within Confederation. As J.F. Conway has observed, "western disaffection, and its continuing expression in regional politics, is the defensive reaction of the people of the West who have fought repeatedly for structural change, only to be defeated each time."[37] The complexities of that fight will be explored in Chapter Four.

In bringing this discussion to a close, we emphasize one point: the argument that institutional flaws lie at the root of the region's economic grievances should not leave the impression that those grievances constitute the totality of regional discontent. The nature of Canadian political institutions is also believed to lead to other forms of discriminatory treatment. As noted above, it is widely believed that the expenditure patterns of the federal government work to the disadvantage of the West, and that broad national programs work more to the advantage of other regions. Although there is a general perception among Canadians that their own province fares less well than others, empirical evidence going back to the 1979 National Election Study shows that this sentiment is more pronounced in the West than elsewhere.[38] It is further believed that the federal government is less sensitive than it should be to the political priorities and symbolic attributes of the West. The comment by former Saskatchewan premier Tommy Douglas that Saskatchewan feels like the "step-child of Confederation"[39] reflects a sentiment felt across the region. Thus we find, for example, that many Western Canadians feel today that the priority their provincial governments have placed on debt and deficit reduction finds only pale reflection in the agenda of the federal government.

CULTURAL DISCONTENT

Once the economic and political grievances surrounding western discontent have been cleared away, there is a residual sense of alienation that can best be described as cultural. In some important way, Western Canadians see themselves as different from those who live outside the region. As Michael Walker, executive director of the Fraser Institute describes it, "western Canadians are a group of people brought together out of a common interest in a common concern about western alienation."[40] They also believe that Western Canadians are seen in stereotypical ways by other Canadians. As in the case of most stereotypes, the objective reality of such perceptions is beside the point. What counts is the role they play as building blocks of regional discontent, a role that is by no means inconsequential. Note, for example, Joe Clark's observation about growing up in High River, Alberta:

... you grew up knowing that you were out on the edge, not at the centre. In one

Percentage of Regional Residents
Receiving Unemployment Insurance or Welfare,
March 1993.

| | % receiving UI | % receiving welfare | per capita UI benefits |
|---|---|---|---|
| Newfoundland | 12.2 | 11.7 | $ 1,335 |
| Prince Edward Island | 12.1 | 9.6 | 1,240 |
| Nova Scotia | 6.8 | 10.7 | 775 |
| New Brunswick | 8.7 | 10.4 | 880 |
| Quebec | 5.6 | 10.3 | 730 |
| Ontario | 3.4 | 12.0 | 465 |
| Manitoba | 3.3 | 7.9 | 440 |
| Saskatchewan | 2.9 | 6.8 | 370 |
| Alberta | 3.4 | 7.4 | 465 |
| British Columbia | 4.2 | 9.2 | 520 |
| Canada | 4.5% | 10.4% | $ 575 |

Source: Edward Greenspon, "Safety Net Snares Many in Disillusionment," *The Globe and Mail*, September 28, 1994, p. A2, and Mark Kennedy, "Putting Pogey to Work," *Calgary Herald*, February 5, 1995, p. A8.

sense, that is a challenging place to be, maybe a better place than at the centre of constraining pressures and traditions. But you knew that the centre had a hold on you, and that the relation was unequal .[41]

What, then, are the stereotypes that feed or reflect regional discontent? Some stem from the days of agrarian settlement in the Prairies, and are best captured by the classic contrast between the country mouse and his city cousin. Others, however, continue to find lively expression in the contemporary and heavily urbanized western environment.[42] We would suggest the following as prime candidates:

- Western Canadians see themselves as more open, friendly, and generous than are the residents of other provinces.[43] (Manitoba licence plates carry the slogan "Friendly Manitoba.")
- Western Canadians are seen by others to be less "cultured," with interests that extend little beyond country and western music and line dancing.

(Among younger Canadians, this latter perception is being challenged by performers such as Jann Arden, Bryan Adams, the Crash Test Dummies, and Spirit of the West.) As Peter C. Newman noted in the gun control commentary mentioned earlier, "most Canadians can never accept the notion that Westerners are anything more than Bubbas out there in the boondocks, oiling their rifles, waiting to spot anything that moves in the bushes, so they can blast it to eternity."[44]

- Western Canadians believe themselves to be more future-oriented than other Canadians. *Vancouver Sun* columnist Barbara Yaffe nicely captures this perception: "In a spiritual sense, I believe the West sees itself as the frontier of Confederation. The new guys on the block, the folks who have the best chance of balancing their budgets and cracking the Asia-Pacific markets. Strong, creative, unpredictable, solid, unfettered by tradition."[45] In the same sense, Western Canadian historians have underscored the utopian character of the early cultural tradition in Western Canada.[46]
- Eastern Canadians value culture more than money, and believe Western Canadians think money *is* culture.
- Western Canadians believe their political leaders are more likely than those elsewhere to be straight-shooters; Eastern Canadians believe Western politicians lack a nuanced understanding of national political realities.
- Western Canadians pride themselves on a casual approach to dress and manners; Eastern Canadians see this as a lack of style and breeding. Here we should note that 58.7 per cent of the Western Canadian respondents in the 1991 Angus Reid survey agreed with the statement that "eastern Canadians think Western Canadians are less sophisticated and educated than themselves."
- Western Canadians see themselves as closer to the natural environment; they are more likely than "effete Easterners" to enjoy the "rugged out-doors."

Again, we wish to stress that the reality of these stereotypes is irrelevant. It does not matter, for example, that Edmonton has perhaps the liveliest theatre scene in the country. Edmontonians believe that this reality is not appreciated outside the region (which it is not), and that it fails to find reflection in such engines of the national culture as CBC Radio and Television.

Cultural tensions are inevitable in a country as large and complex as Canada, and are not to be lamented; they inject important local and regional colour into Canadian life and help energize the cultural environment. Where would we be if everyone loved Toronto and saw Edmonton or Regina as part of the cultural heartland of Canada? By themselves, then, cultural tensions are not problematic, but they can become so when they are ingredients in a more volatile cocktail of political discontent. There is no escaping the conclusion that cultural tensions feed into and reinforce more problematic tensions. For

Perceptions of Saskatchewan

David Smith points out an amusing incident of regional stereotyping. In June, 1994, the remains of a Tyrannosaurus Rex were found in the southwest corner of Saskatchewan. The provincial government, Smith writes, "immediately saw the tourist dollars while the Royal Saskatchewan Museum envisioned the province as one of the richest palaeontological sites in the world. The only sour note to this otherwise exciting event was the *Globe and Mail*'s front page witticism that TR had probably died of boredom in Saskatchewan. Local readers chose to treat this as another sample of the brittle humour that endears Canada's national newspaper to the folk of the hinterland."

David E. Smith, "Saskatchewan 1994," *Canadian Annual Review*, forthcoming.

example, western resistance to the constitutional recognition of Quebec as a "distinct society" taps the belief that Central Canadians fail to acknowledge the cultural life and vitality of the West. In short, Western Canadians are prone to say "if you're not going to recognize the cultural richness of our region, then I'll be damned if I will acknowledge that Quebec is distinct, different, or special." More generally, Western Canadians suspect that Quebec's insistence on protecting its culture is a backhand slap at the West, where it is assumed there are no cultural values to protect.

CONCLUSION

Figure 2.5 presents about as good a bottom-line question for this chapter as we are likely to get, and the pattern of response is unmistakably clear: Western Canadians, by a margin of roughly two to one, do not feel that the West is treated fairly by the rest of Canada. What is also striking to note, however, is the lack of provincial variation in the figure. If the question taps our conventional understanding of western alienation, then we are dealing with a pervasive predisposition; Saskatchewan and Manitoba are not exempt, nor does Alberta stand out as a hotbed of political discontent. This lack of provincial variation persisted when those who felt that the West was not treated fairly were asked the following question: "For some people, the unfair treatment of the West by the rest of Canada is only a minor nuisance which really doesn't affect their lives. Others see this as a major issue which really does affect their lives. Which of these two feelings is closest to your own?" Across the region, 54.4 per cent of the respondents described it as a major issue, with only 38.7 per cent describing it as a minor nuisance. The proportion describing it as a major issue ranged from a high of 57.1 per cent in Alberta to a low of 50.8 per cent in British Columbia.

FIGURE 2.5   Treatment of the West by the Rest of Canada

"Some people feel that, overall, the West has basically been treated fairly by the rest of Canada, while others feel that overall, the West has been treated unfairly by the rest of Canada. How do you feel?"

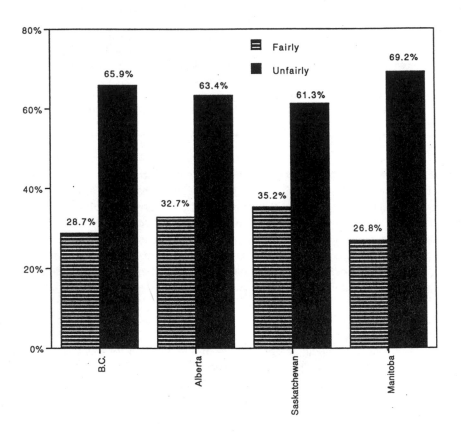

*Source*: Options for Western Canada Study, 1991

**Table 2.1**

Satisfaction with Canada

"In general, would you say you are satisfied or dissatisfied with the direction in which the country is going?"

| | % dissatisfied | | | |
|---|---|---|---|---|
| | *Feb. 91* | *July 92* | *Sept. 94* | *Average* |
| Atlantic | 81 | 71 | 53 | 68 |
| Quebec | 75 | 74 | 61 | 70 |
| Ontario | 84 | 77 | 54 | 72 |
| Prairies | 85 | 80 | 63 | 76 |
| BC | 68 | 76 | 58 | 67 |
| Canada | 80% | 76% | 58% | 71% |

Source: *The Gallup Report*, March 18, 1991; July 30, 1992; and October 3, 1994.

In examining this figure, it is essential to keep in mind that the Angus Reid survey was conducted when Canadians were generally displeased with their political institutions, and when the federal government was plumbing new depths of voter support. As Table 2.1 shows, dissatisfaction with the direction of the country was high at the time. Other Gallup surveys conducted during the period demonstrated that the general discontent reflected in Table 2.1 was also targetted at more specific institutions. For example, the proportion of Canadians who stated that they had either a great deal or quite a lot of respect for the House of Commons stood at only 18 per cent in 1994 and 16 per cent in 1993, compared to 30 per cent in 1989 and 29 per cent in 1984.[47] It is tempting, then, to collapse western discontent into the more general discontent that seemed to characterize Canadians from coast to coast in the early 1990s, and may indeed continue to do so today. This temptation is particularly attractive given the lack of significant regional variation in Table 2.1: Western Canadians do not stand out from the pack in their general level of dissatisfaction with the direction of the country.[48] If, however, western alienation also responds to regionally specific discontent, then the findings of Table 2.1 become not so much an explanation of western alienation as an additional source of concern. Western alienation, we would argue, does more than reflect in a regionally specific way more general currents of political discontent. Rather, it is likely to strengthen those currents, to amplify more general discontent by bringing into play frustrated regional interests and aspirations. If the effect is indeed additive, then the general discontent that Canadians have felt with the political process is a matter of serious concern as we sort through the dynamics of regional discontent and protest.

In order to pull this chapter's story together, it is now useful to step back from the details of public opinion surveys and to draw upon the distinction that David Easton has made among political authorities, the political regime, and the political community.[49] In a broad sense, the *political authorities* are those individuals and parties who hold power at any particular point in time—for example, Pierre Trudeau and the Liberal party during the 1970s and early 1980s. Without doubt, it is the national political authorities and *the public policies with which they have been associated* that have borne the brunt of Western Canadian discontent. As we have seen, and will explore further in Chapter Four, Western Canadians have been relentless critics of the national party system, its constituent parties, and party leaders.

However, Western Canadian discontent has gone beyond political authorities who, after all, are relatively transitory in nature, to embrace the political regime. Easton defines the *political regime* as the rules of the game: the institutions, constitutional documents, and normative conventions that govern political life within a given country. The political regime in Canada would encompass the parliamentary system of government and its institutions, including the Senate and House of Commons; the federal system and its division of powers; and the conventions of responsible government, including strong party discipline and executive dominance. Over the past century Western Canadians have mounted an ongoing, frequently inconsistent, generally ineffectual, but nonetheless often intense attack on the political regime which, in its entirety, has been seen as the source of the region's economic woes. Included in this attack have been proposals to decrease the role of partisanship and to strengthen the role of private members within the House of Commons, to reform the Senate, to devolve greater constitutional authority to provincial governments, to change the electoral system, and to amend the Constitution so as to strengthen the protection of western interests. All of these strategies, and more, will be discussed in Chapter Four.

The *political community* is the most general of the three terms identified by Easton; it refers to those people who live within a defined territory and who share a common identity and set of political institutions. While authorities are the most transitory component of the political system, the community is the least. Despite ongoing demographic turnover and change, it is the community that provides the essential foundation upon which the regime's infrastructure is constructed. To this point, Western Canadian discontent has seldom challenged the national community. Indeed, its primary thrust has been for greater inclusion in that community. In this critical sense, then, Western Canadian discontent is very different from the discontent generated by the nationalist movement in Quebec. Only the latter has sought the dismemberment of Canada and the establishment of a new political community outside the boundaries of the Canadian federal state. Discontented Westerners have wanted in, not out.

Indeed, regional discontent has never coalesced into sizable support for western independence, and thus has not threatened to rupture the national community.[50] If Western Canadians have had a "dream of nation," to use Susan Trofimenkoff's evocative phrase, the nation was Canada and not the West.[51] The western quest was constantly framed in terms of inclusion within the national mainstream; the goal was to achieve political leverage equivalent to the region's contribution to the national economy. And on this point there should be no mistake: Western Canadians have always seen that contribution in very positive, even exaggerated terms. Western Canadians have long felt that they were the ones breaking the soil and building the new country, and it was in the West that the furnace of Canadian nationalism burned the brightest. As W.L. Morton wrote shortly after the end of the Second World War, "the dominant note in the social philosophy of western people has been an unbounded confidence in themselves, a belief that their region was one with a great potential future if the hand of the outside exploiter could only be removed."[52] Alberta Liberal MP David Kilgour provides a contemporary expression of the same sentiment:

> The Western region's overall experience in Confederation to date can be described as buoyancy and confidence encountering continuous disappointment at the hands of outsiders. Full economic and political equality ... continues to elude the region.[53]

However, there is some danger that western discontent may now be questioning the continued existence of the national community, that discontent has reached beyond the political authorities and regime to challenge the political community itself. There is also an even greater danger that the bonds of national unity may be seriously strained by the nationalist movement in Quebec, and by fiscal constraints on national programs and standards. If either is the case, then we may have reached an important turning point for the future of Canada. But, before we draw any firm conclusions, we must look beyond Western Canadian discontent to the more positive visions of the political community that have been promoted in the West. This we will do in the next chapter. We must also explore the dynamics of the relationship between Quebec and the West, for it is those dynamics more than anything else that threaten to rupture the political relationship between the West and the rest of Canada. This we will do in Chapter Five, after which we can return to the future of the West within the Canadian political community.

NOTES

1. Nelson Wiseman, "The West As a Political Region," in Ronald G. Landes, ed., *Canadian Politics: A Comparative Reader* (Montreal: Prentice-Hall, 1989), p. 311.

2. Riel's second rebellion took place in 1885 in what is now Saskatchewan.
3. M.C. Urquhart and K.A.H. Buckley, eds., *Historical Statistics of Canada* (Toronto: Macmillan, 1965), pp. 615-6.
4. David E. Smith, "Saskatchewan 1993," *Canadian Annual Review of Politics and Public Affairs 1993*, forthcoming.
5. In the 1991 census, Native peoples comprised 10.6% of the Manitoba population, 9.8% of Saskatchewan's, 5.8% of Alberta's, and 5.2% of British Columbia's.
6. Barbara Yaffe, "Greening is the rage in B.C.", *Calgary Herald*, January 28, 1995, p. A6.
7. The distinctive ideological character of Alberta is often attributed to a disproportionately large number of American immigrants. However, this impact is difficult to pin down as the Canadian census does not report "American" as an ethnic origin. Therefore the size and destination of American immigration cannot be tracked.
8. "Albertans proud to stick out their rednecks," *Globe and Mail*, June 28, 1994, p. A1.
9. *Ibid.*
10. *Ibid.*
11. Gordon Gibson, "The East Has Finally Caught On—Amazing," *Vancouver Sun*, November 1, 1994, p. A13.
12. For a detailed discussion of Saskatchewan-Alberta differences, see John Richards and Larry Pratt, *Prairie Capitalism: Power and Influence in the New West* (Toronto: McClelland and Stewart, 1979).
13. Ontario's debt, which was close to $90 billion at the end of 1994, was the largest non-national public debt in the world. Anthony Johnson, "Ontario's Debt in World League," *Calgary Herald*, August 22, 1994, p. A1.
14. George Woodcock, *British Columbia: A History of the Province* (Vancouver: Douglas & McIntyre, 1990), p. xi.
15. Joe Clark, *A Nation Too Good To Lose* (Toronto: Key Porter Books, 1994), pp. 73-4.
16. For a detailed discussion, see Vernon Fowke, *The National Policy and the Wheat Economy* (Toronto: University of Toronto Press, 1957).
17. Cited in David E. Smith, *Building a Province: A History of Saskatchewan in Documents* (Saskatoon: Fifth House Publishers, 1992), p. 442.
18. W.A. Waiser, "Saskatchewan," *Canadian Annual Review 1982*, p. 283.
19. Randy Burton, "Romanow urges Chrétien to save Crow," *Star Phoenix* (Saskatoon), March 2, 1995, p. C10.
20. Robert Mansell and Ronald Schlenker, "The Provincial Distribution of Federal Fiscal Balances," *Canadian Business Economics*, Winter 1995.
21. For a thorough discussion of this issue, see Robert M. Campbell and Leslie A. Pal, *The Real Worlds of Canadian Politics* (Peterborough: Broadview Press, 1989), ch. 1.
22. For a discussion, see Jeffrey Simpson, *Faultlines: Stuggling for a Canadian Vision* (Toronto: Harper Collins, 1993), pp. 110-3.
23. Geoffrey Lambert, "Manitoba," in R. B. Byers, ed., *Canadian Annual Review of Politics and Public Affairs 1986* (Toronto: University of Toronto Press, 1990), p. 293.
24. *Alberta Report*, May 6, 1991, p. 52.
25. Clark, *A Nation Too Good*, p.69.
26. This argument is made at length in Kenneth H. Norrie, "Some Comments on Prairie Economic Alienation," in J. Peter Meekison, ed., *Canadian Federalism: Myth or Reality*, third ed. (Toronto: Methuen, 1977).
27. Public opinion surveys show that a majority of Western Canadians support stricter gun controls, but also that support is weaker on the Prairies than it is elsewhere in the country. See *The Gallup Poll*, June 6, 1994.
28. Peter C. Newman, "Gun Control—the CF-18 of the 1990s?" *Maclean's*, May 29, 1995, p. 51.
29. Ted Robert Gurr, *Why Men Rebel* (Princeton: Princeton University Press, 1970).
30. W.L. Morton, "The Bias of Prairie Politics," reprinted in George Melnyk, ed., *Riel to Reform: A History of Protest in Western Canada* (Saskatoon: Fifth House Publishers, 1992), p. 13.
31. The belief that Quebec is the prime beneficiary of western exploitation within Confederation has been reinforced by Reform's success in publicly redefining the "special interests" taking advantage of "the people" through the political system. See David Laycock, "Institutions and Ideology in the Reform Party Project," *Canadian Journal of Political Science*, June 1994.

32. For a more extended discussion of responsible government and party discipline, see Keith Archer, Roger Gibbins, Rainer Knopff, and Leslie A. Pal, *Parameters of Power: Canada's Political Institutions* (Toronto: Nelson, 1995), ch. 5.

33. In the 1993 election, 59% of the seats came from the two Central Canadian provinces.

34. *The Case for Alberta: Addressed to the Sovereign People of Canada and Their Governments* (Edmonton: King's Printer, 1938), p. 376. Ernest Manning, who was provincial treasurer in the government that wrote this report, went on to become a director of the CIBC following his resignation as premier in 1968.

35. The exception was the nine-month Progressive Conservative interlude from June 1979 to February 1980.

36. Alberta alone enjoyed three very able cabinet ministers: former prime minister Joe Clark, deputy prime minister Don Mazankowski, and the Minister of Supply and Services, Harvie Andre.

37. J.F. Conway, *The West: The History of a Region in Confederation* (Toronto: James Lorimer, 1994), p. 321.

38. In the 1979 National Election Study, 29% of Atlantic respondents identified their own province as paying undue costs or receiving less than a fair share of benefits in the Canadian federal state. The figures for the other regions were 38% for Quebec, 46% for Ontario, and 53% for the West. Allan Kornberg, William Mishler, and Harold D. Clarke, *Representative Democracy in the Canadian Provinces* (Toronto: Prentice-Hall, 1982), p. 41.

39. Lewis H. Thomas, ed., *The Making of a Socialist: The Recollections of T.C. Douglas* (Edmonton: University of Alberta Press, 1982), p. 179.

40. Personal correspondence with the authors, July 14, 1994.

41. Clark, *A Nation Too Good*, p. 71.

42. Rural, even bucolic images of the West have by no means disappeared. Note the frustration expressed by former CBC Radio drama producer, Ruth Fraser: "I don't think they [CBC headquarters] realize that we've become urban in western Canada. Toronto has a vision of what we're like, and if we propose a play with an urban setting, they turn it down." *Alberta Report*, July 21, 1986, p. 34.

43. "Other provinces" are in practice Ontario and Quebec; Atlantic Canada does not figure prominently in the minds of most Western Canadians.

44. Newman, "Gun Control," p. 51.

45. Personal correspondence with the authors, June 22, 1994.

46. For example, see R. Douglas Francis, *Images of the West: Responses to the Canadian Prairies* (Saskatoon: Western Producer Prairie Books, 1989), pp. 232-3.

47. *The Gallup Poll*, May 2, 1994.

48. The 1992 Constitutional Referendum Study also found a lack of significant regional variation when respondents were asked to score politicians on a 100-point "feeling thermometer." Scores could potentially range from 100 (very warm or positive) to 0 (very cold or negative), with a mid-point score of 50 being indifferent. Politicians received an average score of 41.5 in Atlantic Canada, 41.6 in Quebec, 39.9 in Ontario, and 38.7 in the West.

49. David Easton, *A Framework for Political Analysis* (Englewood Cliffs, N.J.: Prentice-Hall, 1965).

50. For an example of the radical fringe of western discontent, see John Barr and Owen Anderson, *The Unfinished Revolt* (Toronto: McClelland and Stewart, 1971). See also Larry Pratt and Garth Stevenson, eds., *Western Separatism: The Myths, Realities and Dangers* (Edmonton: Hurtig, 1981).

51. Susan Mann Trofimenkoff, *The Dream of Nation: A Social and Intellectual History of Quebec* (Toronto: Macmillan, 1982).

52. W. L. Morton, *The Progressive Party of Canada* (Toronto: University of Toronto Press, 1950), p. viii.

53. David Kilgour, *Uneasy Patriots: The West in Confederation* (Edmonton: Lone Pine, 1988), p. 262.

# CHAPTER THREE

# Western Visions

It would not be surprising if, after the last chapter, the reader was left with the impression that the West as a political region can best be understood as a complex bundle of unrelenting grievances. However, while there is no denying the importance of such grievances to Western Canadian politics, they should not blind us to the existence of more positive regional values and aspirations. It is possible to identify western "national visions" that have deep historical roots and reflect a principled position on the nature of political life. These visions address not simply the place of the West within the Canadian federal state, but also the nature of *Canada* as a political community.

More specifically, we can identify a particular western vision that has been brought into reasonably sharp focus in recent years. It is one that emphasizes the equality of individuals, provinces, and regions, and which embraces many of the contemporary tenets of populism. But this vision is by no means uncontested within the West, much less within the country as a whole. As we will see, it runs counter to alternative western visions which are also deeply embedded in the region's history, and which have found reflection in a series of western protest movements. Nonetheless, it pulls together a number of important themes in Western Canadian political life, and provides many individuals with a principled platform from which to view constitutional and public policy debates. Furthermore, it has considerable potential appeal beyond the West, for it is built upon and amplifies values which are of central importance to many and perhaps most Canadians *outside Quebec*. In this sense, and for better or worse, it can be seen as a prototype for a new form of Canadian nationalism that might emerge should Quebec withdraw from Confederation.

It is not our intent to endorse or champion any of the western visions that will be outlined in this chapter. While we do not deny that the various visions have some personal appeal, our primary intent is to articulate and explain those visions, and to show how they are anchored in the broader value structure of the Canadian political community; we leave it to others to take up the crusade.[1] Given that comparisons with Quebec are involved in much of the discussion to come, it is important to stress at the outset that we do not want to leave the impression that the values reflected in western visions are alien to residents of Quebec. Canadians all live within a liberal-democratic environment, and as a consequence share a broad set of values and beliefs. Thus, when contrasts are drawn, they are contrasts between the political cultures of Quebec and the West, or more specifically between the "centres of gravity" of those cultures. The values which anchor the political culture in Western Canada are not without support in Quebec; they are simply less central to the political culture of that province.

Our first task is to sketch in the national visions that have come to dominate the political landscape in Western Canada. We will do this by looking at regional perspectives on individual equality and multiculturalism, provincial equality, and regional equality. The discussion of regional equality will provide the opportunity to discuss the relative weight that Western Canadians attach to provincial, regional, and national identities, and the extent to which that weight varies across the four provinces. The chapter will then move to a discussion of populism and its contribution to the western national visions. In conclusion, we will discuss some of the important points of tension between the national visions that are coming to dominate the western landscape and more conventional national visions. As Western Canadians have found in the past, it is not always easy to reconcile their view of the political world with that held by other Canadians.

THE EQUALITY BEDROCK

If there is one word of paramount importance to political discourse in Western Canada, it is *equality*. It is also a word of many and complex meanings, one that is often used rather loosely and without reference to the very nuanced theoretical debate over the meaning and nature of equality in western democratic states. Sometimes the intended reference is to the *equality of individuals*, and in this sense the meaning is very close to how most Canadians would articulate the core value of the Charter of Rights and Freedoms.[2] Sometimes the word takes on more mathematical or formal precision, as when Western Canadians talk about provincial equality within a reformed Senate, or the constitutional equality of the federal and provincial governments. Sometimes it refers simply to justice or fairness: when Western Canadians talk about *regional equality*, they are talking about something more fundamental than the weights assigned to territorial units within the central institutions of the state. And sometimes equality blends into majoritarian notions of *populism*, into the belief that the will of the people can be established in some rough way by counting heads equally.

Now there is nothing strange or idiosyncratic about the prominent role of individual equality in the Western Canadian political culture. This form of equality is of foundational importance to virtually all liberal democratic states; its expression in the American Declaration of Independence—"We hold these truths to be self-evident: That all men are created equal..."— provided an enduring template for liberal democratic thought. The equality of individuals finds expression in the notion of one person, one vote; in such documents as the Charter of Rights and Freedoms; and in the principle of equal treatment before the law. Then what, if anything, sets Western Canadians apart from those living in other regions of the country? The distinction may come from the relatively un-nuanced stance taken by Western Canadians toward equality issues: the contemporary stress is on the equality of rights, and to a degree on the equality of opportunity, but with less stress placed on equality of condition. As we will see, the proponents of equality of condition have by no means disappeared, but their voice within the regional political culture has been subdued relative to historical experience. Western Canadians may also stand apart through three other factors: the emphasis individual equality receives within the regional political culture; the reluctance to temper the equality of individuals with other political values; and the entanglement of the commitment to individual equality with regional opinion both toward Quebec, which will be examined in Chapter Five, and toward multiculturalism, which will be addressed here.

## *Multiculturalism and individual equality*

At first glance, one might expect Western Canadians to be strongly supportive of multiculturalism and the growing importance it has assumed in constitutional design, institutional structures, and public policy. After all, Parliament's 1971 adoption of official multiculturalism owed a great deal to the political pressure brought to bear on the federal government by multicultural communities in Western Canada.[3] Multiculturalism reflected the rich array of ethnic communities that had settled the West and shaped so much of the frontier experience. In that sense, it was almost synonymous with the nature of the Western Canadian society, or at least the Prairie society. Note, then, the 1973 endorsement of multiculturalism given by Saskatchewan premier Allan Blakeney:

> Ours must be a province where people of every cultural background have full access to their own ethno-cultural heritage; to economic and political affairs, and to the future developments in all of these spheres in Saskatchewan, without discrimination. Such a society will not only guarantee that all our residents, wherever they came from, have a sense of full participation in the affairs of this province, but may also provide an attractive climate for new Canadians who we hope will join us in the decades ahead.[4]

However, this multiculturalism emerged against an historical background in which ethnic diversity was seen as a problem as much as an asset. The prairie West was filled with a new polyglot population holding to a multitude of different religious creeds. It was a population, moreover, with shallow social and political roots, supplied with only the makeshift social institutions of early settlement, and engaged in an uncertain and frequently precarious economy. The scene was nicely captured in 1909 by J.S. Woodsworth, who went on to become the region's most renowned progressive critic:

> Within the past decade, a nation has been born. English and Russians, French and Germans, Austrians and Italians, Japanese and Hindus—a mixed multitude, they are being dumped into Canada by a kind of endless chain. They sort themselves out after a fashion, and each seeks to find a corner somewhere. But how shall we weld this heterogeneous mass into one people? That is our problem.[5]

The challenges of social and political integration were immense, and therefore the multiculturalism that came to be articulated in the West stressed the equality of *individuals* rather than groups. It argued for race-blind and ethnicity-blind public policies and political processes; it was assimilationist by nature, envisioning a community in which all individuals would enjoy the same rights, freedoms, and opportunities. The "cultural mosaic" and "melting pot" were not antagonistic conceptions in the West but rather two faces of the same coin. Ethnic diversity was to be celebrated and preserved, but it was not to provide the foundation for the *political* community. Within that community, the equality of individuals was to prevail.

It is for this reason that multiculturalism could be supported within a region that also produced the champions of an unhyphenated Canadianism. The first and most famous was the Rt. Hon. John Diefenbaker, prime minister of Canada from 1957 to 1963. His advocacy of "One Canada" was integral to his electoral appeal in the West, and to his rejection by the Quebec electorate following a brief flirtation in the 1958 election. Diefenbaker's biographer, Thomas Van Dusen, argues that Diefenbaker's national vision had deep roots within the history of the prairie provinces:

> "One Canada" was born on the prairie trails; in the fire and comradeship of World War I; in the section shacks of the railroad among immigrants with unpronounceable names; in the dreams of a new world free of prejudice and discrimination. It was a Canada where every citizen possessed the same rights of citizenship; where the heritage of all was preserved, even that of the majority; where every citizen enjoyed the same chance to get ahead, regardless of what part of the country he lived in, what his name might be, or where his parents came from. It was a Canadianism respecting differences, not erecting them into impassable barriers.[6]

A cynic might suggest that Western Canadians have fallen well short of this ideal, and that Van Dusen's history strays from the empirical record, but to do so would be to miss the point. The power of visions to drive the political process and to shape our perceptual world is not dependent upon their fidelity to reality. Diefenbaker was able to articulate a core value in the regional political culture, and *to promote that value as the foundation for a broader form of Canadian nationalism*. National visions weave together myths as much as they do objective realities, and Diefenbaker was a master weaver. When he championed "One Canada" in his 1967 fight against his own party's adoption of a "deux nations" position on Quebec, Diefenbaker was speaking for an audience that extended well beyond the West. Although Diefenbaker was branded as a reactionary Westerner for his opposition, Pierre Trudeau was to use essentially the same rhetorical position to crush the Progressive Conservatives in constitutional debates throughout the late 1960s and 1970s.

Diefenbaker's vision of an unhyphenated Canadianism finds contemporary expression in Western Canadian scholarship[7] and, more importantly, through the western-based Reform Party of Canada. Like Diefenbaker, Reform calls for an unhyphenated Canadianism and equality for all Canadians.[8] As Jeffrey Simpson points out, Reform leader Preston Manning's "vision of unhyphenated Canadianism sprang from Prairie experience, where groups respected cultural heritages but eventually sublimated them into the greater community."[9] Hyphenated Canadianism is rejected because it emphasizes differences at the expense of our common ground. Note, for example, Manning's lament that Canada's national symbol has become the hyphen rather than the maple leaf:

> [Canada's] federal politicians talk incessantly about English-Canadians, French-Canadians, Aboriginal-Canadians, ethnic-Canadians, but rarely about "Canadians period." It has become patently obvious in the dying days of the 20th century that you cannot hold a country together with hyphens.[10]

This lament, which can be directed as much to other Canadians as it can to Westerners, is linked in turn to the approach taken by Manning toward the Canadian mosaic:

> Let individuals, groups, lower levels of government if necessary, be responsible for cutting and polishing the individual pieces. But let the government of Canada be responsible for the common background on which these pieces are to be stuck, and the glue that holds them together. The elements of that common background and glue may include the rule of law, an open economy, an efficient public administration, guarantees of artistic and other freedoms, and shared symbols such as the national flag and anthem.[11]

Manning goes on to argue that "the role of the federal government should be neutral toward culture just as it is toward religion."[12] In these views, Manning is very close to the spirit of John Diefenbaker's "One Canada." His address to the 1994 Annual Assembly of the Reform Party could well have been delivered by Diefenbaker himself:

> I tell you, if we were rebuilding the national house, its foundation would be built on the bedrock of equality of provinces and equality of citizens, so that your

standing with the government rests solely on your Canadian citizenship, not on your race, language, culture, gender, creed, or where you live in the country. We should all be treated as equals in our own house![13]

Manning's "folkloric" approach to multiculturalism[14] also appears, at least to his critics, to be at odds with Canada's official and constitutional commitment to multiculturalism. However, it is by no means clear that he is at odds with public sentiment in Western Canada. Figure 3.1 shows that in British Columbia, Alberta, and Saskatchewan, there is little support for special protection for multicultural communities. Even in Manitoba, where such support is the strongest, a plurality of respondents in the 1991 Angus Reid survey disagreed with the statement that "people from different cultures who have immigrated to Canada need special protection for their human rights."

The point to stress is that the equality of individuals and support for multiculturalism, as the latter was traditionally conceptualized, could and did co-exist comfortably within the political culture of Western Canada. However, contemporary multiculturalism has taken on new features which may challenge that co-existence. The preservation and celebration of difference have assumed greater importance, and have been projected with greater force into the political arena. Multiculturalism has also become closely associated with public programs and expenditures, and with state intervention into the social order. In this sense, multiculturalism runs up against fiscal constraint and ideological currents of neo-conservatism which work to erode and shrink the state. (The most convenient angle of attack for the opponents of multiculturalism, one that avoids any discussion of principles, is to argue that we simply cannot afford multicultural programs while coping with chronic deficits and debt.) And, it must be admitted, the initial support for multiculturalism emerged at a time when the greatest number of immigrants were white and came from European countries. The contemporary context for multiculturalism is quite different and, not to their credit, some Western Canadians have undoubtedly opposed multiculturalism because it is seen to promote a racial transformation they resist.

At the same time, to associate this last predisposition with the West alone would not only be a disservice to the region; it would badly misread the dynamics of immigration and multiculturalism politics elsewhere in the country. As Figure 3.2 shows, national support for increased immigration has been weak throughout the past two decades, and the plurality opinion in the most recent Gallup polls has been that levels of immigration should be reduced. Moreover, the last Gallup poll in the series depicted in the figure, a poll conducted in December 1993, shows that Western Canadian opinion fits the national pattern.[15] There was little regional variation in the proportion of respondents favouring increased immigration; the proportion ranged only from 9 per cent in Quebec to 12 per cent in Ontario and British Columbia. If we look at the proportion favouring a decrease in immigration, we find greater

FIGURE 3.1   Support for Special Protection For Immigrants

"Do you agree or disagree that: people from different cultures who have immigrated to Canada need special protection for their human rights?"

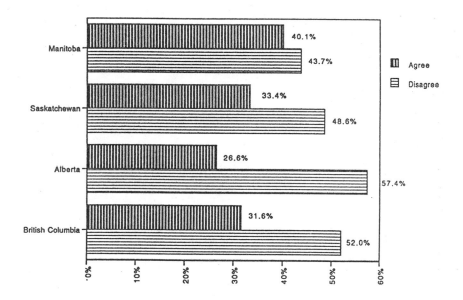

*Source*: Options for Western Canada Study, 1991

FIGURE 3.2   Public support for Immigration

"If it were your job to plan an immigration policy for Canada at this time, would you be inclined to increase immigration, decrease immigration, or keep the number of immigrants at about the current level?"

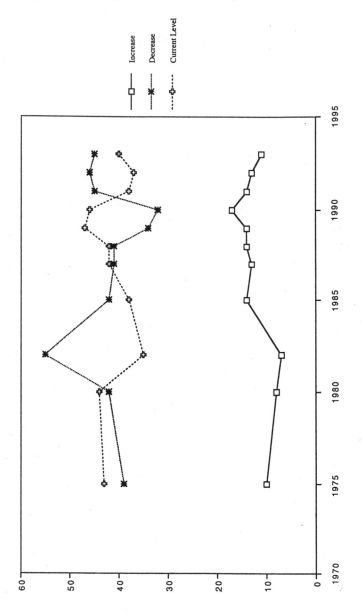

*Source*: The Gallup Poll

variation but no clear evidence that Western Canada stands apart: the proportions ranged from 35 per cent in Atlantic Canada to 41 per cent on the Prairies, 43 per cent in Ontario, and 51 per cent in both Quebec and British Columbia. In this case, then, Western Canadian opinion is not at odds with opinion in the country at large.

In bringing this discussion of individual equality and multiculturalism to a close, we should stress a number of important points. First, while we would argue that the commitment to individual equality is a foundational characteristic of the contemporary regional political culture, this has not always been the case. The historical treatment of racial and ethnic minorities in the West stopped well short of any such ideal: well into the 1950s, for example, Asians in British Columbia faced a restricted provincial and local franchise, the University of Manitoba had ethnic quotas in its professional faculties, and some Winnipeg and Vancouver suburbs prohibited Jews and other ethnic groups. Second, support for the formal equality of individuals is not unique to the West. Respondents to the 1992 Constitutional Referendum Study were asked if they agreed or disagreed with the statement that "the constitution should make no distinctions among individuals, for we are all Canadians." While 92.2 per cent of Western Canadian respondents agreed, so too did 89.4 per cent of those from Ontario and 94.6 per cent of those from Atlantic Canada. Only in Quebec did agreement fall off significantly, to 76.6 per cent. As Table 3.1 shows, moreover, Western Canadian opinion on employment equity programs is not greatly out of line with the national pattern. Opposition to such programs is strong across the country, and Western Canadian opposition simply amplifies national sentiment.

Finally, and perhaps of greatest importance, there has been no clear consensus within the West as to whether the emphasis should be on the formal equality of individuals, often expressed as equality of opportunity, or on equality of condition. While we suspect that support for the former prevails at the present time, support for the latter has deep roots within the region and still has a substantial impact on public policy debates. Regional visions grounded in a commitment to equality of condition found expression in the early Progressive movement, and in the electoral support that the CCF/NDP enjoyed, if somewhat sporadically, in three of the four western provinces.[17] Perhaps the clearest manifestation of support for equality of condition came from the pioneering efforts by the Saskatchewan government to establish a comprehensive public health care system, efforts that were eventually to find national expression in the Canada Health Act. In 1947, Saskatchewan established the first hospital insurance plan in Canada, and then in 1960 introduced a comprehensive, prepaid medical care program covering the entire provincial population. In defending this latter initiative in the Saskatchewan legislature, Premier T.C. Douglas made it clear that equality of opportunity required some measure of redistribution, and therefore some endorsement of equality of condition:

**Table 3.1**

Regional Support for Employment Equity Programs

"As you may know, women and minority groups are often under-represented at the management level of government and the broader public service. Do you believe governments should actively attempt to hire more women and minority group members for management positions, or should governments take no action whatsoever and hire new employees based solely on their qualifications?"

|          | *Hire more women and minority group members* | *Hire on basis of qualifications only* | *Don't Know* |
|----------|------|------|------|
| Atlantic | 27   | 71   | 3    |
| Quebec   | 28   | 64   | 9    |
| Ontario  | 20   | 75   | 5    |
| Prairies | 17   | 79   | 4    |
| BC       | 11   | 85   | 4    |
| Canada   | 21%  | 74%  | 6%   |

Source: *The Gallup Poll*, December 23, 1993.

In the final analysis, the greatness of this province will depend on the extent to which we are able to divert a reasonable share of the wealth production of this province to make it available to raise the standard of living of our people, and to give them a reasonable measure of social security against old age, against sickness and other catastrophes. Above all, the greatness of Saskatchewan will depend on the extent to which we are able to use the resources of this province to provide greater equality of opportunity, and to make this a place where people can enjoy more abundant living.[18]

This vision continues to enjoy strong support across the region, as provincial governments have found when they have closed hospitals and reduced medical care in the face of budget deficits. It also finds expression in some of the region's most articulate academic voices. Note, for example, J. F. Conway's call for a new national policy: "All Canadians, regardless of region of residence, must be assured that the nation is dedicated not just to a basic national minimum level of well-being but to programs that will lead to a genuine equality of condition for all."[19]

These alternative visions, one presenting a hard-edged view of individual equality extending only to equality of opportunity, one supporting equality of access to social programs and therefore, to a degree, equality of condition, are not unique to the West. They represent ideological currents, and indeed tensions, found across Canada and other liberal democratic states. But within the West, they are often seen to be epitomized by Alberta, in the former case, and Saskatchewan in the latter. Saskatchewan is seen as the spiritual homeland of the CCF/NDP, the founder of medicare, the supporter of comprehensive and national social programs, while Alberta is seen as the home of Reform, and the slash-and-burn, neo-conservative budget-cutting of Ralph Klein. Such characterizations, however, are less accurate than we might assume. The differences between the Saskatchewan Conservative governments of Grant Devine and the NDP governments that preceded and followed Devine are as great as the differences between the two provinces. Devine pushed the kind of privatization agenda that people associate with Alberta, whereas in Alberta the Conservative governments of Peter Lougheed and Don Getty were at the same time still indulging in massive social and economic development spending.

So while there clearly are conflicting visions in the West, there is limited utility in trying to lodge such visions within specific provinces. The policy debates they generate ripple throughout the region, and across the country. While provincial leaders may still emphasize differences in order to better position their own agendas, their articulation of provincial differences must be taken with a grain of salt.[20] At the very least, such differences should not conceal intraprovincial differences which may rival and even surpass those among provinces in Western Canada.

*The equality of provinces*

A second component of the national visions articulated by Western Canadians is found in the assertion of *provincial equality*, an assertion that has taken a number of forms. It has been most clearly expressed in regional support for a Triple-E Senate (discussed in greater detail in the next chapter), in which each and every province, regardless of its population, would have the same number of senators. This numerical definition of provincial equality has been buttressed by references to the American and Australian Senates, within which each state is entitled to the same number of senators—two each for the American states and twelve each for the Australian states. As Triple-E supporters point out, both Australia and the United States have huge population disparities between the largest and smallest states, but this has not prevented the formal and numeric equality of states within the national legislative chamber designed to provide regional representation. Here we might also note as an aside that political debate in parts of the West is more inclined to draw upon non-Canadian sources and examples than is debate elsewhere in the country. (In a January 1995 speech, and in a manner unlikely to be replicated by politicians outside the region, or even outside the province, Alberta Premier Ralph Klein described himself as "Newt North," a reference to the newly installed Republican Speaker of the U.S. House of Representatives, Newt Gingrich.[21]) Western supporters of Senate reform, and particularly those in Alberta, do not consider it unpatriotic to suggest that Canadians might have something to learn from over two hundred years of American federal experience.

It is not surprising to find that support for an *equal* Senate is relatively strong in the West. The 1992 constitutional referendum survey asked respondents to choose between two Senate reform options: an equal Senate, where all provinces would have the same number of seats, and an *equitable* Senate where large provinces would have more seats than smaller ones. As Figure 3.3 shows, support for an equal Senate was greatest in the West, although the difference between Western and Atlantic Canadian respondents was negligible. Similar results came from a June 1992 Gallup survey which asked the following question: "Do you favour changing the Canadian Senate so that each province has an equal number of senators, or do you think the provinces with larger populations should have more seats in the Senate?" The proportion supporting an equal Senate ranged from 57 per cent on the Prairies and 54 per cent in Atlantic Canada, to 51 per cent in British Columbia, 34 per cent in Ontario, and 29 per cent in Quebec.[22] It is also interesting to note that although the campaign for an equal Senate has been most closely and most persistently associated with Alberta, support for the equal option was not stronger in that province at the time of the 1992 constitutional referendum study: 66 per cent of Alberta respondents supported the equal option, as did 65 and 70 per cent of those in Manitoba and Saskatchewan, respectively. Only in British Columbia, the province that would be disadvantaged by equality, did support for the equal option fall off to 56 per cent.

To a degree, numerical equality among the provinces is captured in the first part of the general constitutional amending formula adopted in 1982. More specifically, the formula states that constitutional amendments require the approval of Parliament and seven of the ten provincial legislative assemblies. All provinces receive equal treatment in this part of the formula; no province is singled out by name and no province has a veto, two critically important features of the amending formula for the West.[23] (However, the formula then goes on to state that the seven consenting provinces must contain at least fifty per cent of the national population.) The other parts of the amending formula, which require unanimous consent for changes to such things as the office of the Queen, the composition of the Supreme Court, and the amending formula itself, can be seen to endorse provincial equality in that each and every province must consent. Earlier proposals for an amending formula, including the 1971 Victoria formula, were rejected (at least by Alberta) because they failed to recognize provincial equality.[24] Regional equality was not seen as an adequate substitute, especially when two provinces, Ontario and Quebec, were portrayed as regions unto themselves.

The belief in provincial equality has taken a less numeric form in assertions about the appropriate relationship between governments in the Canadian federal state. Provincial governments in the West have endorsed a theory of federalism in which the federal and provincial governments are equal and co-or-

FIGURE 3.3    Senate Reform Options

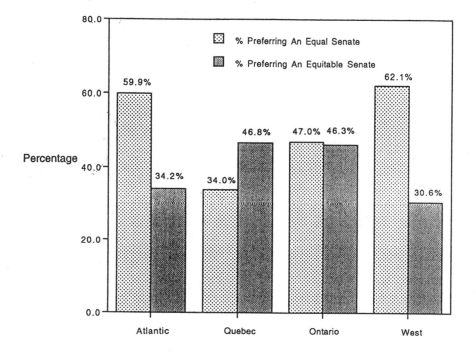

*Source*: 1992 Constitutional Referendum Survey

dinate, rather than unequal and hierarchical. The two governments are seen as sovereign within their own spheres, and therefore equal. This viewpoint has been particularly associated with Alberta and, less explicitly, British Columbia. Thus the Alberta government has vigorously resisted any reference to "levels" of government, or to other terminology that might suggest that provincial governments are "below" and thereby subordinate to the federal government. The preferred terminology is "orders of government," a phrasing that does not imply any hierarchical ranking. As Braid and Sharpe point out, Peter Lougheed reinforced this position by insisting that his provincial ministers would meet only with their ministerial counterparts in Ottawa, not with their deputy ministers, and that provincial deputy ministers would meet only with their Ottawa counterparts, and not their subordinates.[25] With respect to this last form of provincial equality, the position of western provinces is very much in line with that of Quebec. In both cases we find an associated emphasis on provincial autonomy and provincial rights. It should also be noted that this form of equality implies that no one government can speak for Canada, that only the eleven federal and provincial governments, in *concert*, can do so.

Support for the different notions of provincial equality varies considerably across political parties in the West, and across the region. With respect to the former, provincial equality has been an important part of the Reform creed since the party's founding, and Reform's 1994 national assembly stated the party's first principle in the following terms: "We affirm our commitment to Canada as one nation and to our vision of Canada as a balanced federation of equal provinces and citizens." However, provincial equality has never played a prominent role in the regional wings of the Liberal, New Democratic and Progressive Conservative parties. With regard to variation within the region, support has been noticeably stronger in Alberta than to the east or west of that province. Perhaps not coincidentally, Alberta is the only province with close to a tenth of the national population, and therefore the notion of provincial equality makes some mathematical sense. (Alberta is either the largest of the small provinces or the smallest of the large.) Manitoba and Saskatchewan combined have fewer people than Alberta alone, and thus any argument for provincial equality must ground itself on premises other than representation by population. British Columbia is the largest of the four western provinces, and for that reason alone its residents may find the notion of provincial equality less appealing. A Triple-E Senate, for example, would provide fewer BC senators than the province would receive on the grounds of population alone. But in a more general sense, few British Columbians believe that the province has an equal. The more common belief is that God broke the mold after She made BC, the "supernatural" province.

It is worth noting that support for the formal equality of the provinces does not automatically translate into support for *substantive* equality. In British Columbia, where support for formal equality has been substantial if somewhat weaker than on the prairies, equalization payments have been a frequent target for provincial governments of all stripes. Social Credit premier W.A.C. Bennett often spoke out against equalization payments to other provincial *governments*, arguing that such payments were misdirected:

> The money was collected by the federal government and the provinces and they poured it out into provincial governments. I'd go visit these provincial govern-ments and I'd see in their offices the enormous staffs they had, all with our money.... I only oppose these equalization payments because they were going to the wrong people. They were going to the provincial governments so they could let political contracts—a lot of patronage for their party. I wanted this money, all of it, to raise the standards of the poor and to help the working poor.[26]

In 1995, NDP premier Mike Harcourt picked up on the same themes when he suggested a planned reduction in equalization payments.[27] On this issue, opinion in British Columbia differs sharply from that on the Prairies.

*Regional equality*

The quest for regional equality is no more and no less than a demand for fair-ness. Note, for example, the following passage by Don Braid and Sydney Sharpe:

> Westerners want only one small thing from Canada - Equality. They long to be equal partners in a truly united land that includes Quebec, pleases the Maritimes and deals fairly with all provinces.... regional equality is the one basic demand of most westerners.[28]

Notions of regional equality are not based on numerical considerations. No one suggests, for example, that equal regional representation in the contem-porary Senate—Ontario and Quebec each has 24 Senate seats, as do the four western provinces combined, while the four Atlantic provinces have 30 seats—is an appropriate response to Western Canadian concerns. Nor, for that matter, do the proponents of equal provincial representation in a Triple-E Senate see any tension between this proposal and *regional equality*. The demand for regional equality stems from the belief, buttressed by the evidence presented in Chapter Two, that the political system and therefore the econom-ic system work systematically to the advantage of the two Central Canadian provinces and to the disadvantage of the West. In short, the demand for regional equality is the demand to redress the sources of western alienation. "Treat us equally" means "treat us fairly."

The concern for regional equality has not been based on the assumption that the West is different and therefore worthy of protection, but rather on the desire of Westerners to be an influential part of the national mainstream. Note, for example, the following comment by one of the most pre-eminent histori-ans of Western Canada, W.L. Morton: "The West has been defined as a colo-

Barbara Yaffe,

"Western Provinces Remain Rivals"

"Like debutantes, they sit along side one another at the western edge of the country. They are young, beautiful, wealthy. They are also scratch-your-eyes-out rivals....

B.C. and Alberta generally keep to their respective sides of the Rockies, cosy in the knowledge that if any provinces can afford to separate from that debt-ridden blob called Canada, it is they. While the two have much in common, few kisses get carried across the way by chinook winds. These are fiercely independent jurisdictions that hurl nasty words across mountain passes as appropriate occasions arise....

Just plain folks got into the act last summer when writer Ric Dolphin, who had moved from Vancouver to Edmonton, attacked prevailing stereotypes. Edmonton is supposed to be cold, boring and ugly, he wrote. 'Vancouverites refuse to believe anyone could enjoy living in anything other than the green playhouse they call home.'

The truth, he wrote, is that Vancouver is damp, soggy and depressing and its less-than-friendly citizens feed ferociously on praise they get for the ocean/mountain thing as if they personally had a hand in helping God design the topography."

Yaffe is a columnist with the *Vancouver Sun*. This column was published in the *Calgary Herald*, January 21, 1995, p. A6.

nial society seeking equality in Confederation. That equality has been sought in order that the West should be like, not different from, the rest of Canada."[29] Morton's comment suggests that Western Canadians of his era were not trying to impose a new national vision as much as they were trying to buy into the existing national vision of Sir John A. Macdonald. This line of argument has been picked up more recently and transformed by George Melnyk, who suggests that when Western Canadians describe themselves as "alienated" they are taking on an identity defined from the outside. In discussing the evolution of the term *western alienation*, Melnyk writes:

> It was not important what Westerners felt about themselves; it was important that they were *alienated from* the centre where all goodness lay. It was Westerners who were alienated, while Central Canadians were not. The burden of deviancy was the West's.[30]

The demand for regional equality has been an important political theme in the West. However, the inclusion of regional equality in western national visions rests on the assumption that the region as a whole has some reality, and some relevance in the minds of Western Canadians: in other words, that it is more than a geographical or statistical artifact. If Westerners attach greater importance to the province in which they live than to the region as a whole, then notions of *regional* equality other than the basic demand for fairness can be expected to play a relatively minor role in western visions. This, we suspect, is generally the case. Note, for example, the following comment by Vancouver journalist and media personality Rafe Mair:

> .... I am not now and have never been a westerner. I am a British Columbian who knows little if anything about the public mood in Manitoba, Saskatchewan and Alberta except to note that they are east of the Rockies, though perhaps not as much so as others.[31]

Similar views have been expressed by Barbara Yaffe, columnist for the *Vancouver Sun*:

> As someone who has lived across Canada, from Newfoundland to B.C., I'd have to say that the national community is of less concern here than it has been everywhere else I've lived. There's a real sense of independence in B.C. and a lack of preoccupation with things to the east because of that independence. The western vision of Canada, to some extent, is characterized by the oft-used phrased "back east." It's a big lump, in that direction, beyond the mountains, populated by people who don't know us and certainly don't hear us.[32]

The available empirical evidence offers mixed support for a regional consciousness. As we will see shortly, Western Canadians are far more likely to identify with Canada or their province than with "Western Canada." However, the 1991 Angus Reid study suggests that a regional consciousness should not be written off too quickly. Respondents were asked the following question: "Some people think that, in some important respects, the West should be thought of as a unique region in Canada. Other people do not think the West is a unique region. What do you think?" By margins of nearly two to one, respondents across the West saw their region as unique. Differences among the provinces were negligible: the proportion seeing the West as a unique region ranged only from 66.0 per cent in British Columbia and 64.2 per cent in Alberta to 64.1 per cent in Saskatchewan and 62.5 per cent in Manitoba. It is possible, of course, that respondents in different provinces attached different definitions to "the West." In this context, historian Gerald Friesen has suggested that a restricted regional consciousness—restricted, that is, to east of the Rockies—played an important role in the evolution of the three Prairie provinces.[33]

There is, then, potential confusion between regional and provincial identities. If British Columbians see themselves as "Western Canadians," this
should not be taken as unequivocal evidence of emotional affiliation with the
residents of Alberta, Saskatchewan, or Manitoba; it may well be that "the
West" to which they refer starts at the British Columbia/Alberta border and
ends at the Pacific. Conversely, Albertans have been guilty of rhetorical imperialism, casually projecting provincial grievances onto the region as a whole.
Albertans, often to the irritation of their neighbours, have been quick to speak
for the region as a whole and to wrap "the West" around provincial interests.
Their rage at the 1980 imposition of the National Energy Program, for
instance, was expressed as regional rage. The NEP was portrayed as an attack
on the West even though reactions to the program were much more moderate
outside Alberta than they were inside. The residents of Manitoba in particular
were largely indifferent to the negative impacts of the NEP, given that the
province has no petro-chemical resources. Although Manitoba premier
Sterling Lyon spoke out against the NEP, he was driven more by strategic considerations than by outrage among his constituents. Here it might also be
noted that the Reform party is often guilty of rhetorical imperialism when it
speaks for "the West" despite its electoral weakness in Manitoba and
Saskatchewan.

As we will argue in greater detail in Chapter Five, the West as a political
region comes to the fore at times of crisis, and particularly when the country
is confronted by demands from Quebec for constitutional change. Although
political rhetoric in such cases is often framed in the context of "the West,"
this should not blind us to the strength of provincial identities and the underlying heterogeneity of the region. Nor should any of this discussion blind us
to the *strength* of national identities across the West. Extensive public opinion
evidence shows that national identities are as strong in the West as they are
elsewhere in the country, and indeed in many cases are even stronger. Given
that this finding is of fundamental importance in understanding the national
character of western visions, it is worth taking the time to examine the empirical evidence in some detail.

In the 1974 and 1979 national election studies, respondents were asked to
indicate their level of support for Canada and their province on a 100-point
thermometer scale. In both cases, western scores for Canada were at or slightly above the national average (even when the relatively low scores of Quebec
respondents were put aside) and western scores for Canada were higher than
the ratings for the respondents' provinces.[34] A 1977 national survey asked
respondents whether they thought of themselves first as a Canadian or as a
provincial resident; western respondents across the board were more likely to
cite a Canadian identity than were respondents from any province other than
Ontario.[35] In 1989, Decima Research also asked a national sample of 1,500
respondents whether they thought of themselves first as a Canadian or as a citizen of their province. When provinces were ranked by the percentage of

respondents stating a Canadian rather than provincial identity, Alberta ranked sixth, British Columbia fourth, Saskatchewan third, and Manitoba second.[36]

More recent surveys tell essentially the same story. Figure 3.4 shows that respondents in the 1991 Angus Reid survey overwhelmingly opted for a Canadian identity even though the national government was very unpopular at the time. The Reid survey also showed only modest differences among respondents in the four western provinces: 80.7 per cent of Manitoba respondents chose the Canadian identity as the most important compared to 77.7 per cent of British Columbia respondents and 73.8 per cent of Alberta and Saskatchewan respondents who made the same choice. Two 1991 surveys by Gallup provide some comparable context for the Angus Reid findings. The first asked respondents if their "primary allegiance" was to Canada or to their provincial or local community. Regional variations were quite pronounced, with the proportion opting for Canada ranging from 32 per cent in Quebec to 57 per cent in Atlantic Canada, 64 per cent on the Prairies, 69 per cent in British Columbia, and 74 per cent in Ontario.[37] The second Gallup survey asked respondents "how proud they were to be a Canadian." In this case, the proportion stating that they were "very proud" to be a Canadian ranged from 40 per cent in Quebec to 66 per cent on the Prairies, 69 per cent in Ontario, 71 per cent in British Columbia, and 75 per cent in Atlantic Canada.

Two final pieces of evidence are worth mentioning as we draw this discussion to a close. In the 1992 national referendum survey, respondents were asked to score "Canada" on a 100-point feeling thermometer. There were no significant differences among Atlantic, Ontario, and Western Canadian respondents in the mean scores assigned to Canada, and no significant differences among respondents from the four western provinces. The most recent evidence comes from a late 1993 survey conducted by Decima Research. As Figure 3.5 shows, Western Canadian respondents are marked by the relative strength of their national identities, and by the modest variation within the region.

The empirical picture is clear. Across a variety of measurements taken at a variety of times, Western Canadians demonstrate relatively strong attachments to Canada. If the West stands apart from the rest of the country in any way, it is in the strength rather than the weakness of those attachments. Moreover, there is not a great deal of variance within the West in terms of the strength of national attachments. At the very least the empirical evidence provides no indication that Canadian attachments or identities weaken as one moves west from Manitoba to British Columbia.

*Populism*

The regional stress on the equality of individuals lends itself readily to a complementary enthusiasm for populism. As a style of political discourse and as an ideological framework, populism has deep roots within the prairie West.[38]

FIGURE 3.4   Provincial, Regional, and National Identities

"Which of these identities—Provincial, Western Canadian or Canadian—is the most important to you?"

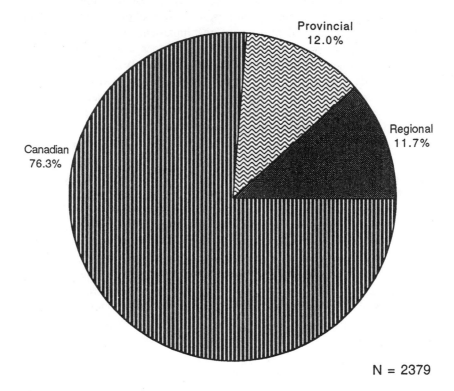

N = 2379

*Source*: Options for Western Canada Study, 1991

FIGURE 3.5   Provincial and Canadian Identities

In a late 1993 survey conducted by Decima Research for *Maclean's*/CTV, 1610 respondents were asked if they thought of themselves as a Canadian first, or as a resident of a particular province or region. As the figures show, a very strong majority of Western Canadians identified themselves first as Canadians. Only 17% of B.C. respondents, 16% of Alberta residents, 7% of Saskatchewan, and 1% of Manitoba respondents opted for a provincial identity.

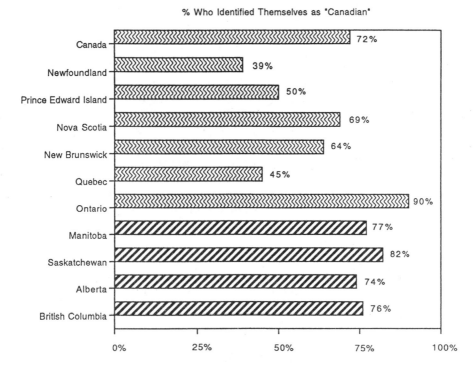

% Who Identified Themselves as "Canadian"

Historically, it grew out of the perceptions that external elites were exploiting the region, and that the political system was tilted towards those holding economic wealth and power. As Sydney Sharpe and Don Braid explain, "populism is a western tradition because of the frustration people feel toward a perceived colonial power structure in Ottawa."[39] Initially, it drew heavily from earlier populist sentiment and movements in the American West and Midwest.[40] References by Alberta Social Credit in the mid-1930s to the "50 bigshots" who controlled Canadian financial institutions, and therefore political institutions, captured a more general regional theme. Populist sentiment was fed by the frustration Western Canadians found with regional representation in the House of Commons, where western MPs appeared to become so entangled in partisan interests and constraints that voters back home were forgotten or ignored. Means were therefore sought to make MPs more receptive and responsible to their constituents, and less beholden to national parties centred in Ontario and Quebec. Thus we saw the early appeal to non-partisanship, and to instruments of direct democracy such as recall.[41] Early populist sentiment also reflected cultural tensions between the agrarian West and the urban East. While it would be an exaggeration to say that regional mythologies pitted the "prairie yeomen" against the "effete elites" of Central Canada, at times they came close.

As an approach to politics, populism is designed to loosen the control of political elites, and to vest legislative power in the hands of "the people."[42] It strives for the equality of individuals within the political process, and proposes a series of devices to give effect to that equality. Thus populism is associated with the use of plebiscites, referendums, and citizen initiatives, and at times with mechanisms for the recall of sitting politicians.[43] These devices are in turn premised on individual equality, with each person's vote carrying an identical weight, and on the assumption that conventional party politics fails to translate popular preferences into public policy. Support for populist principles and devices has always been stronger in Western Canada than it has been elsewhere in the country, just as it has been stronger among the western states south of the border. This support, moreover, has been manifest across the region, although at some times it has been stronger in some provinces than in others. British Columbia now has recall legislation in place, and in 1991 Saskatchewan had a referendum on whether abortions should be financed by the provincial medical insurance plan. Both Manitoba and Alberta have enacted legislation requiring a referendum before taxes can be increased or new taxes instituted, and British Columbia has enacted legislation that permits legislative initiatives.[44] It was the commitment by Alberta and British Columbia, and initially Quebec, to hold a provincial referendum on any constitutional amendments that forced the 1992 national referendum on the Charlottetown Accord.

The history of British Columbia provides useful examples of populist politics. Certainly the early Social Credit movement and its leader, W.A.C.

Bennett, provide fine examples. As Bennett's biographer, David Mitchell, explains, Social Credit supporters "viewed themselves as ordinary folk, pitted against large, organized, impersonal forces directing their lives. Their early haphazard efforts gave the movement a kind of populist image which was one of the reasons for its eventual success in British Columbia."[45] Social Credit's 1956 campaign slogan was "Progress not Politics," and in this context Mitchell notes that "Bennett was the first B.C. politician to successfully seek office by censuring the essence of his trade."[46] However, it is important to stress that British Columbia illustrates a more general regional predisposition toward populist politics. As Figure 3.6 shows, for example, support for citizen-initiated referendums is widespread and does not vary significantly from province to province. In the 1991 Angus Reid survey, 80.3 per cent of the regional respondents said they would like to have used citizen-initiated referendums to vote for or against the GST, 76.8 per cent to vote for or against the Free Trade Agreement, and 75.5 per cent to vote for or against the Meech Lake Accord.

The strongest contemporary advocate of populism is the western-based Reform party, pledged as it is to respect "the common sense of the common people." As Jeffrey Simpson notes, however, Reform has also expanded the traditional populist understanding of, and opposition to, elites:

> The middle class resentments that simmer in the Reform Party are directed against elites, to be sure, but also against welfare cheaters, uppity social activists, feminist rhetoricians and other minoritarian pleaders, who by dint of access to the media and politicians' desire to curry favor, twist public priorities to assist themselves, leaving excessive burdens of taxation and burgeoning regulations to restrict the freedoms of the hard-pressed, overtaxed and underappreciated majority.[47]

Populism fits neatly within the context of western alienation. It has an intuitive appeal to people who see themselves victimized by distant economic and political elites who have little understanding of or sympathy for the "grass roots." Populism seeks to bridge the presumed gulf between rulers and the ruled, a gulf that for Western Canada has always existed in a geographical sense. (Westerners are quick to refer to the "Ottawa disease," an affliction that overcomes Western MPs soon after they arrive in Ottawa and which wipes out any memory of regional concerns or empathy for regional interests.) As Preston Manning has written:

> Whenever populism has become a force to be reckoned with in Western Canadian politics, it has been energized by "western alienation"—a conviction shared by generations of Western Canadians that their region and interests have not achieved equality with the constitutional and economic interests of Quebec and Ontario, and that systemic change is necessary to achieve such *equality*[48] (emphasis added).

FIGURE 3.6   Support for Citizen Initiated Referendums

"Do you support or oppose, on principle, the notion of allowing citizens to pass or repeal laws directly through citizen initiated referendums?"

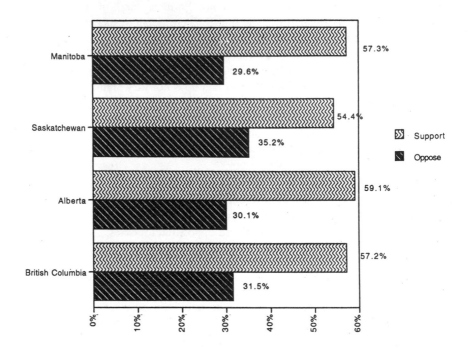

*Source*: Options for Western Canada Study, 1991

Current manifestations of populism

The spirit of populism is neatly expressed by Vancouver journalist and author Robert Mason Lee. In a column that attacked the support of "syrupy-voiced elites" for asymmetrical notions of federalism, Lee employed the classic rhetoric of populism. It is interesting to note, however, that average Quebecers were also brought under the populist umbrella:

"As far as the elites are concerned, Canada must tolerate a degree of asymmetrical federalism to accommodate its linguistic and cultural duality. This is a high-priced notion that no one would wear on the streets. Westerners with children enrolled in French immersion do not need the elite to interpret for them the burying of the English language in Quebec. Neither do Quebecers need the elites to explain away the burning of their flag in English Canada. *They do not need to have their feelings described for them. They do not need their words spoken for them. They do not need their grievances dismissed.* They need a restored sense of respect and fairness." (emphasis added)

Robert Mason Lee, "Please don't tell Westerners to shut up about the referendum," *The Globe and Mail*, September 17, 1994, p. D2.

In Manning's case, the linkage between populism and the quest for regional equality is direct and explicit.

This is not to imply, of course, that all Western Canadians are populists. Very successful leaders such as Peter Lougheed adopted a personal style well-removed from populism, and John Diefenbaker was a strong defender of British parliamentary tradition and institutions, neither of which displayed much empathy for the methods of direct democracy which are so central to populism. (In an October 20, 1949 speech to the House of Commons, Diefenbaker said "No Canadian can but be proud that through the warp and woof of our Constitution are the golden threads of our British Heritage.")[49] Nonetheless, populism has become an important part of the Western Canadian political culture, and on the contemporary scene right-wing populism has found forceful expression through the Reform party.[50] It is also embedded in the more general culture of the West, one that puts considerable stress on social informality.

*Summary*

To this point in the chapter, we have argued that reasonably coherent Western Canadian national visions can be articulated, visions based on the equality of individuals, the equality of provinces, fair and thus equal treatment for the regions, and support for more populist forms of political decision-making that would mitigate the effects of an electoral and party system tipped towards Central Canadian interests. However, this is not to suggest that these visions are shared by all Western Canadians, or even recognized by all. Nor are we suggesting that they enjoy uniform support. Moreover, it must be recognized that inconsistencies may exist. There is, for example, considerable tension between provincial equality and the democratic equality of individuals. How can one justify treating Ontario and Saskatchewan as equals, given that the former has a population almost ten times as large as the latter? Provincial equality can be achieved only through individual *inequality*, as Ontario voters have been quick to recognize when confronted with proposals for a Triple-E Senate.

Other lines of cleavage exist among the national visions articulated in the West. John Diefenbaker, for example, was populist in style without endorsing any structural change to parliamentary government. His was a populism of the spirit rather than of the political process, and he would have had little patience for Reform's support for referendums and initiatives. (Diefenbaker said that dogs knew best what to do with public opinion polls.) Diefenbaker was also an unequivocal supporter of a strong national government; he "believed in a national community of individuals, a collective vision, the popular will, majority rule, and anti-elite reformism."[51] This was a stance that ran counter to the province-building ambitions of provincial leaders such as W.A.C. Bennett and, after Diefenbaker's prime, Peter Lougheed. In the case of Lougheed, this province-building orientation led to a durable intergovernmental alliance with Quebec, one that was to find some reflection in the partisan coalition that Brian Mulroney forged within the Conservative party between the West and nationalist elements in Quebec. In a March 1977 speech to the Alberta Progressive Conservative party, then-premier Lougheed drew some parallels between the positions of Alberta and Quebec on Canadian confederation:

> ... just as Albertans want more control over their destiny—primarily for economic reasons—Quebecers, I sense, also want more control over their destiny, essentially for cultural and linguistic reasons. Hence, just as Albertans want more government decisions made in Edmonton than in Ottawa, I think Quebecers, for different reasons, but somewhat similar motives, want more government decisions made in Quebec City, and fewer in Ottawa.[52]

Many Western Canadians have been willing to ride the coattails of the Quebec nationalist movement so long as any gains by Quebec were generalized to the West. As Robert Mason Lee observes, "since Canada remains a federation of equal provinces, any advance made by Quebec is an advance for all."[53] Others, however, including Saskatchewan's Allan Blakeney, have feared that the decentralist ambitions of Quebec could harm the strong feder-

Looking forward, not back

Western Canadian visions of the country are fixed firmly on the future, not on the past. In this sense, the West is still very much a pioneer region; little weight is attached to where people have come from, and a great deal is attached to the dreams they might be able to achieve together. While historical grievances are not forgotten—scratch an Albertan and memories of the NEP rush to the surface, as do long-standing grievances about freight rates in Saskatchewan—they are not central to the regional political culture.

This assertive attachment to the future, and the corresponding diminution of the past, does not play well in parts of the country with a deeper sense of history and a strong identification with particular historical events. In an article written for *The Globe and Mail*, Ray Conlogue lamented the failure of English Canadians to acknowledge Quebec's founding trauma, the Conquest of 1759. English Canadians, he argued, will never be able to come to grips with the contemporary dynamics of Québécois nationalism because they fail to understand how deeply rooted that nationalism is, and how profoundly the trauma of the conquest has been embedded in Quebec's political culture:

English Canadians are so uncomfortable with this subject that they invariably steer the conversation toward disapproving homilies about those who let themselves be trapped by history, or irrelevant comparisons with the miseries suffered by immigrant Ukrainians. From Westerners one often hears that Quebec whines about its history in order to extract more money from the rest of us.

Conlogue both captures and misses an important point. Western Canadians do disapprove of those who let themselves be trapped by the past, but this disapproval cannot be dismissed as "homilies." It is integral to the regional political culture, and it is as legitimate as any fixation on a relatively minor clash of British and French imperial armies on the Plains of Abraham more than 200 years ago.

Ray Conlogue is the Quebec arts correspondent for *The Globe and Mail*. His article, "A dialogue of the deaf between the conqueror and the conquered," was published on January 21, 1995 (p. D3).

ation that was so important to the trading interests of the West.[54] In short, there is considerable diversity within the West, as we should expect, but this does not negate the existence of recognizable *regional* visions. Nor does it negate the potential national appeal of visions based on conceptions of equality which have some universal application. However, elements of the western vision have collided with other values within the Canadian political culture; we have seen, for example, how this has been the case with contemporary multiculturalism. Unfortunately, this has not been the sole source of tension.

THE "DOWNSIDE" OF EQUALITY

There is no question that "equality" is a positive value. As Barry Cooper suggests, the equality of provinces "is the underlying formal principle of federalism, just as equality of citizens is the underlying formal principle of liberal and constitutional democracy."[55] Indeed, it is difficult to think of parties or leaders who have marched to victory under the banner of "inequality." However, the equality of persons and provinces as articulated in the West has run up against other values within the Canadian political community. The regional articulation has resulted in a fundamental schism between the West and Quebec, one to which Chapter Five is devoted in its entirety. Nor does equality fit easily with the aspirations of Aboriginal communities in the West, aspirations which reject the blanket application of individual equality and majority rule. Institutional expression for provincial equality has not been easy to achieve, and tensions exist between populism and deeply rooted Canadian attachments to responsible, representative government. At the same time, it should be stressed that the conflicts surrounding equality do not necessarily follow regional lines. It is worth remembering, for example, that Reform won more votes in Ontario in the 1993 general election than it did in the three Prairie provinces combined.

*The elusive goal of provincial equality*

One might think that the non-hierarchical orientations that provincial governments in the West have taken towards federalism—orientations which stress the formal equality between the federal and provincial governments—would find a receptive audience in Quebec. Certainly the view that federalism should be seen as comprising two orders of government, each sovereign within its own sphere, is by no means alien to political discourse in Quebec. Westerners and Quebecers might differ over the relative size of the two sovereign spheres, with the latter preferring a substantially larger sphere for provincial governments, but they are in basic agreement on the nature of federalism. Intrusions by Ottawa into provincial jurisdictions have been hotly contested in each case, although opposition has not been uniform across the West: resistance to the strict application of the Canada Health Act, for instance, has been much more pronounced in Alberta than it has been elsewhere in the region. Despite such basic similarities, however, opinions in Quebec and the West diverge dramatically when it comes to equality among the provinces. The dominant western view that Quebec is one province among ten equals is not accepted within political or constitutional discourse in Quebec. (Nor, incidentally, has it been accepted by Joe Clark: "In Canada, equality has never meant uniformity—and, indeed, uniformity often means inequality, because it does not take account of real differences. That rule applies to provinces as well as to people.")[56] The equality that is embraced in Quebec is between *nations*, or cultural communities, and not among provinces. Even the broader notion of regional equality finds little positive resonance within Quebec, where the portrayal of Quebec as one region among four or five is seen to negate its distinctive nature.

Needless to say, the residents of Ontario have little appetite for provincial or regional equality. It is true that Ontario politicians, and particularly former premier Bob Rae, have begun to distinguish between the provincial interests of Ontario and the national interests of Canada, a distinction that Ontario politicians were prone to reject in the past. (The residents of Ontario and the West have long shared a perception that the interests of Ontario and Canada are inseparable; they just differ on whether this is a good thing!) Thus Rae promoted a strategy of "Ontario first," and, with important exceptions on the constitutional front, was reluctant to subordinate provincial interests to national concerns. Rae was particularly incensed at the manner in which federal transfer payments have discriminated against Ontario, an anger shared by the premiers of Alberta and British Columbia with respect to their provinces. None of this, however, is likely to lead to an acceptance of a vision of Canada based on ten equal provinces, or even on equal regions. Ontario's demands for fair treatment may appear to echo perennial themes in the West, but these demands will not lead to any relinquishment of the demographic clout that Ontario asserts within the Canadian political process.

But if a western vision based on the formal equality of individuals, provinces, and regions is unattractive to Ontario and Quebec, what about the alternative vision that emerged from the Progressives and the CCF/NDP, one that emphasizes national programs and substantive equality among individuals and provinces? Will the "Saskatchewan model" provide a better fit with the national political culture, or at least that culture as reflected in Ontario and Quebec? Unfortunately, the answer may well be no. The only pan-Canadian vision with any significant appeal in Quebec is one featuring radical decentralization and the abandonment of national standards and programs, a vision completely at odds with those articulated by western leaders such as Allan Blakeney, M.J. Coldwell, John Diefenbaker, Tommy Douglas, and Mel Hurtig. As the federal Liberal government, backed by 98 Ontario MPs, moves toward greater fiscal restraint, the offloading of social programs, and a "flexible, evolving federalism" designed to appeal to the soft nationalist vote in Quebec, it is by no means clear that Ottawa is moving into line with western visions of Canada and the federal state.

Special Status for Quebec?

Two of the most controversial provisions of the 1992 Charlottetown constitutional accord were the recognition of Quebec as a distinct society and the guarantee that Quebec's representation in the House of Commons would not fall below 25 per cent of the total number of seats. In the 1992 Constitutional Referendum Survey, Western Canadians opposed both provisions, but they did so in almost equal proportion to the residents of Ontario and Atlantic Canada.

|  | Atlantic | Quebec | Ontario | West |
|---|---|---|---|---|
| % agreeing that Quebec should be recognized as a distinct society | 32.7 | 74.7 | 34.2 | 29.3 |
| % agreeing to a 25 per cent seat guarantee for Quebec in the House | 17.1 | 47.7 | 17.0 | 12.0 |

In short, there was little that was distinctive about the western reaction. Admittedly, Western Canadians displayed less support for either provision, but the differences were not dramatic. (A Gallup survey conducted in September 1992, showed that English Canadian support for the seat guarantee ranged from 25% in Ontario to 23% in Atlantic Canada, 19% on the Prairies, and 15% in British Columbia.)[57] Indeed, there was greater variation within the West than there was among the three English Canadian regions. Support for the recognition of Quebec as a distinct society, for example, ranged from a high of 35.6% in Manitoba to a low of 17.9% in neighbouring Saskatchewan.

## Populism and representative democracy

Although populism is likely to have considerable and perhaps even growing appeal in the years to come, it is not without its problems as an approach to government. Populist devices such as referendums or initiatives may polarize the political community, severely inhibit the pursuit of political consensus and compromise, may be vulnerable to capture by special interest groups, and may over-tax the participatory interests of the electorate. However, our intent here is not to address the general pros and cons of populism,[58] but rather to point out that populism does not fit easily with the value that the Canadian political culture, and particularly its elite articulation, attaches to representative democracy.

Parliamentary democracy in the Canadian case is representative democracy. While voters have the power through elections to determine which party forms the federal or provincial government, they generally have no direct power to shape legislative decisions between elections.[59] Their policy power is indirect, and comes from the capacity to "throw the bastards out" if the government pursues policies that are out of line with the popular will. It also comes from the somewhat weaker ability to provide the winning party with a "mandate." It is assumed, however, that between elections political elites will, in their own self-interest, govern in the best interests of the electorate. We speak through our elected representatives and we have the power to judge their performance at the polls, but we cannot govern in their place. Thus democracy is representative rather than direct.

The support of Canadians for representative democracy has certainly been shaken from time to time. There have been some quite dramatic differences between the policy preferences of elected politicians and those of their constituents: the ongoing debate over capital punishment, the imposition of the Goods and Services Tax, and a good measure of post-1982 constitutional politics provide but three examples. It should also be noted that direct democracy has come into play in some of *the* most important decisions that Canadians have faced. The 1949 decision by Newfoundlanders to enter Confederation, the 1980 rejection of sovereignty-association in Quebec, and the 1992 rejection of the Charlottetown Accord were all taken through provincial or national referendums. Moreover, there is survey evidence of broad public support for some tenets of populist thought. A fall 1990 national survey of 2,947 respondents found that 65 per cent agreed with the statement that "I'd rather put my trust in the down-to-earth thinking of ordinary people than the theories of experts and intellectuals," and 74 per cent agreed that "we could probably solve most of our big national problems if decisions could be brought back to the people at the grass roots."[60] (In neither case were there significant regional differences.) However, we would contend that populism enjoys much greater support from political leaders in the West than it does from leaders elsewhere, and that it is more deeply embedded in the western political culture. Thus to the extent that national visions articulated in Western Canada place a heavy emphasis on populism, they may find the reception of the national electorate to be cool at best.

The western affection for populism also runs somewhat counter to the demographic position of the West within the Canadian federal state. If *national* policy were to be set by populist mechanisms such as initiatives and referendums, the Central Canadian electorate would carry the greatest weight. Ontario's population alone is almost a third larger than that of the four western provinces combined, and Quebec's population is more than 80 per cent of the Western Canadian population. In total, 62.3 per cent of the national population lives in Ontario and Quebec. Therefore populism itself would do little to address the long-standing regional perception that the national political system is tipped toward the interests of the Central Canadian electorate. Indeed, populism might well strengthen rather than correct this bias, a possibility that western supporters of populism have been slow to appreciate. Populism would not have prevented the National Energy Program, and in fact might have given the NEP much greater legitimacy. Nor would it ensure that federal largesse flows equally to the West.

There is little question that the West's enthusiasm for populism strikes a threatening chord in Quebec. Populism is inherently a majoritarian philosophy with limited appeal for minority populations. The inclination is to count heads equally, and to set aside racial, ethnic or linguistic differences among those heads. Populists assert the equality of individuals, and by so doing deny political importance to demographic differences among individuals. Quebecers, and for that matter francophones across the country, are a permanent minority and therefore are unlikely to be enthusiastic about populism, as applied to federal politics. (Populism *within* Quebec is another matter entirely, as the use of constitutional referendums illustrates.) And yet, by the same logic, populism should also be problematic for the minority of the national population living in Western Canada. The distinction, and it is an important if not widely appreciated distinction, is that the differences of opinion between those living inside and outside the West are likely to be less pronounced than are the differences between the Quebec and non-Quebec populations. In this sense, populism is less threatening to the interests of Western Canadians than it is to Quebec residents.

Finally, it should be recognized that populist sentiment in the West can blend into a form of *secular fundamentalism* that sits uneasily with a national political culture emphasizing moderation, compromise, and accommodation. Reform party leader Preston Manning refers to this concept in the following terms: "Secular fundamentalists—and I do not use the term in a derogatory sense—include people who hold uncompromising convictions on everything from the role of women in society to environmental conservation."[61] Tom Flanagan links this to the "monism" or "philosophy of oneness" expressed in Manning's thought and Reform's philosophy.[62] As Flanagan points out, monism is problematic in a pluralistic society in which sharply defined group interests are an inevitable feature of the political landscape. However, if there is a problem here, it is by no means confined to Preston Manning and Reform. The broader regional appeal of secular fundamentalism is evident in the large number of Western Canadians who have moved from positions of religious leadership to active political life: William "Bible Bill" Aberhart, M. J. Coldwell, Tommy Douglas, the Rev. Phil Gaglardi, Ernest Manning, and J.S. Woodsworth only begin the list. When the CCF promised to build "the new Jerusalem," and when the Reform party is described as "storming Babylon,"[63] Canadians outside the West may well see regional protest as a challenge to the moderate, pluralistic and secular national mainstream.

CONCLUSION

In this chapter, a careful reader will have noticed a fair degree of overlap between some of the "western visions" that we have tried to articulate and the platform of Reform. This overlap is not coincidental, for a good part of Reform's success has come from its ability to identify and articulate long-standing regional values. Preston Manning's own visions of the West and of the country spring from a close reading of Western Canadian history, and Canadian history more broadly defined. He knows the regional mythology inside and out, and has been able to weave it throughout his party's platform. Although Manning has found greater resonance in Alberta and British Columbia than he has in Saskatchewan or Manitoba, he is not without broad regional appeal.

As we noted in an earlier chapter, the founding (and now discarded) slogan of Reform—The West Wants In!—is the best encapsulation of western alienation available. The first of twenty-one principles outlined in the party's 1991 Blue Book addressed the issue of Senate reform and in so doing nicely captured the themes of this chapter: "We affirm to establish a Triple E Senate in the Parliament of Canada—that is to say, a Senate which is Elected by the people, with Equal representation from each Province, and which is fully Effective in safeguarding regional interests."[64] The Reform party also provides the primary although by no means exclusive vehicle for populist sentiment in Western Canada, and the Blue Book statement on populism is one of the best available definitions of the creed:

> We believe in the common sense of the common people, their right to be consulted on public policy matters before major decisions are made, their right to choose their own leaders and to govern themselves through truly representative and responsible institutions, and their right to directly initiate legislation for which substantial public support is demonstrated.

Reform is the latest in a long series of regional protest movements, and it is not surprising that considerable overlap exists between the party's platform and the more general articulation of western grievances and aspirations.

At the same time, it is important to distinguish between "Western Canadian visions" and the more specific political vision associated with the Reform party. Reform is not the West, although it has deep roots within the region, and the West is not Reform, although Reform has provided a potent vehicle for regional discontent and aspirations in British Columbia and Alberta. There are important aspects of Reform policy that are not intrinsic to the national visions articulated in the West. Reform's stress on fiscal constraint, and upon a neo-conservative agenda that would radically shrink the size of the Canadian state, is not the inevitable product of western experience. Although it does have some bloodline connection to Alberta's Social Credit experience in the 1930s, it finds pale reflection in the historical experience of Manitoba and Saskatchewan. The problems of the debt and deficit are national problems first and foremost, and some of the most vigorous proponents of fiscal constraint and the accompanying neo-conservative agenda have come from the Central Canadian business community. Provincial governments in the West have not been particularly associated with either fiscal constraint or a neo-conservative agenda. The NDP has done well in provincial elections across three of the western provinces, with Alberta being the clear exception. But even in the case of Alberta, the dominant pattern of public policy until the last few years has been characterized by extensive public spending and state intervention. In this respect, the recent advocacy of small government and fiscal constraint by Ralph Klein is an anomaly on the provincial landscape; neither was pursued during the oil-fed heydays of the Peter Lougheed and Don Getty governments. Thus Reform's determination to "shrink the political domain" is not a reflection of western tradition.[65]

Nor, for that matter, does the anti-statist populism of Reform share much with the broader populist tradition in the West. As David Laycock explains:

> These contemporary right-populists have adopted a neo-conservative redefinition of the public sphere that is antithetical to earlier populist democracy in one crucial aspect. It insists that citizens' problems of economic insecurity and social alienation result from too much rather than too little public participation.[66]

Laycock goes on to argue that "in the new right/right-populist model, basic decisions about public issues are to be made on the model of informed, individual consumers in a competitive market."[67] The contrast with more traditional populist discourse in the region could not be clearer:

> Most earlier prairie populists promoted active citizenship in closely knit communities, expressed in social and economic as well as political forms. Co-operatives, public education and political organizations were all elements of meaningful citizenship.[68]

The Reform party has succeeded in pulling a good deal of traditional western alienation into focus, and in providing alienated Westerners with a vehicle for political expression. However, Reform's appeal reaches well beyond the sphere of western alienation. As Laycock explains, Reform support in the 1993 election "relied more on a set of themes and assumptions that gave the regional mistreatment theme special appeal in the West, *and remind us that alienation from the modalities of public life exists independently of region*" (emphasis added).[69] Reform's assault on special interests, which Laycock takes to include "feminist lobby groups, native organizations, organized labour, multicultural, linguistic and ethnic groups, the management of most

Crown corporations and state agencies, and public sector unions,"[70] is by no means regional in character or potential appeal. The point, then, is that the Reform phenomenon is both smaller and larger than the West.

The distinction between Reform policy and western visions more broadly defined is important for a number of reasons. First, any close association between the two permits the opponents of Reform—and they are legion—to dismiss Western Canadian visions of any form. This dismissal is already commonplace in contemporary political debate, to the distress of Western Canadians who are not affiliated with Reform, and of Reform supporters who feel, correctly, that their visions, concerns, and aspirations are being placed beyond the pale of legitimate political debate. The relationship is frustratingly reciprocal. Reformers are tarred with the Western Canadian brush—"the Reform vision is regional, not national"—and Western Canadians trying to articulate a new national vision are tarred with the Reform brush—"Western Canadian nationalism is simply a smokescreen for a neo-conservative agenda that is foreign to Canadian values." The second reason to draw a distinction between western and Reform visions is that as Reform tries to expand its base of support into Ontario, and even into Quebec, it will begin to shed its close identification with regional symbols and values. We can therefore expect to see the nationalization of Reform, and thus the continued disengagement of Reform and regional "national visions."

But what do we conclude, then, about the national appeal of these "western national visions"? For the most part, the national visions articulated by Western Canadians are not idiosyncratic in character. Once again, the values they incorporate are by no means alien to Canadians living outside the West, and indeed may have universal appeal. As Bercuson and Cooper note, "The formal principle of Canadian political life, as of other liberal democratic regimes, is equality."[71] In many respects, western visions can be seen as a regional *amplification* of values held by many Canadians from sea to sea to sea. At the same time, other values which have come to the fore as Canadians have tried, unsuccessfully, to grapple with the place of Quebec within the Canadian federal state have been understated in the West. For example, there is less emphasis placed on binational visions of the country, or on the equality of founding peoples; such concepts are dismissed in the West as theoretical artifacts lacking any foundation in the regional experience. Therefore the western expression of Canadian nationalism has not recognized the distinctive character and aspirations of Quebec; it has sought inclusion for the West, but not on terms that would accommodate the inclusion of a constitutionally distinct Quebec. To the contrary, it has been associated with national visions which have little currency in Quebec, a reality that is clearly illustrated in the recent debate over Senate reform. Admittedly, provincial governments in the West supported the Meech Lake Accord and then, with considerably less enthusiasm, the Charlottetown Accord, but in both cases they failed to carry their own electorate with them.

Peter Lougheed's National Vision

In a speech to the 1981 Annual Convention of the Alberta Progressive Conservative Party, then-Premier Peter Lougheed sketched in two competing national visions:

There are two very different visions of Canada being put forward today, and these two visions are in conflict. One vision of Canada is that we are too small and weak to prosper unless we are fully controlled at the centre, of course, being Ottawa.... There is another vision of Canada. This vision recognizes that the prosperity in one region is beneficial to all regions. It is a vision of Canada where bitterness, frustration and confrontation are replaced by an awareness that there has to be equity, there has to be fairness between the regions, wherever you live in Canada and whatever the colour of your political map.... It is a vision of Canada where there are strong checks and balances in this nation, with strong provinces and strong provincial governments.... It is clearly my personal vision.

Cited in David G. Wood, *The Lougheed Legacy* (Toronto: Key Porter Books, 1985), pp. 242-3.

Many of the various threads of Western Canadian nationalism were pulled together in the proposal for a Triple-E Senate. The first E—Equality—captured the emphasis placed on the formal equality of provinces within the constitutional structures of the Canadian federal state. The second E—Elected—captured the emphasis on populism, and a suspicion of the elite-dominated politics of executive federalism. The third E—Effective—captured the belief in a strong national government; a rejuvenated upper house was seen as a means to increase the legitimacy and therefore ultimately the political authority and clout of the national government. Unfortunately, this institutional expression of the region's national vision also brought the conflicting aspirations of Quebec and the West into bold relief. As we will see in Chapter Five, the "national" vision that came to dominate Quebec during the same period rejected provincial equality, rejected the call for an elected upper chamber, and sought to weaken the government of Canada rather than rendering it more effective. Thus so long as Senate reform is used to express and capture the national visions of Western Canadians, the region will remain at loggerheads with political opinion in Quebec. Nor, for that matter, will it be possible to secure significant political support in Ontario.

The extent to which regional visions are anchored in the more general value structure of the national political community reinforces our point that western visions go beyond regionalism. It is a form of *Canadian* nationalism that has taken hold in the West, and it addresses the nature of Canada as much as it addresses the concerns of the West. The belief in individual equality, in the formal constitutional equality of the provinces, in fair play among regional interests, and in more democratic means of political decision-making are not without appeal across Canada. Yet to the frustration of Western Canadians, national visions emerging from the West are not accepted elsewhere as legitimate national visions. In this context, Braid and Sharpe refer to "the smug belief of Ontario politicians that they speak for all English Canada and that Ontarians truly care about the nation, while others are self-centred regionalists."[72] Here we should also note the western sensitivity to the charge that regional support for strong provincial governments necessarily means a weak national government. To the contrary, Western Canadians assert that "federalism, to be effective, needs strong provinces,"[73] and that to be strongly attached to British Columbia or Manitoba is an expression of a strong attachment to *Canada*.

The national visions which dominate Western Canadian political thought have encountered two primary obstacles. First, they have failed to find institutional expression within the Canadian federal state. Second, and clearly related to the first, they have come up against very different national visions emanating from Quebec, visions which to date have carried more weight within the national political system. The following two chapters address these obstacles in turn.

NOTES

1. For example, see David Bercuson and Barry Cooper, *Deconfederation: Canada Without Quebec* (Toronto: Key Porter Books, 1991).
2. We acknowledge that the Charter also incorporates group rights, but would argue that most Canadians still see individual equality as the core value.
3. This point is discussed in greater detail in Chapter Five.
4. Cited in David E. Smith, *Building a Province: A History of Saskatchewan in Documents* (Saskatoon: Fifth House Publishers, 1992), p. 200.
5. Cited in Jean Bruce, *The Last Best West* (Toronto: Fitzhenry and Whiteside, 1976), p. 14.
6. Thomas Van Dusen, *The Chief* (Toronto: McGraw-Hill, 1968), p. 69. Diefenbaker was eight years old when his family left Ontario in 1903 to homestead in Saskatchewan.
7. For example, see George Melnyk, *Radical Regionalism* (Edmonton: NeWest Press, 1981), p. 74.
8. Preston Manning, *The New Canada* (Toronto: Macmillan, 1992), p. 298.
9. Jeffrey Simpson, *Faultlines: Struggling for a Canadian Vision* (Toronto: Harper Perennial, 1994), p. 123.
10. Cited in Andrew Stark, "English-Canadian Opposition to Quebec Nationalism," in R. Kent Weaver, ed., *The Collapse of Canada?* (Washington, D.C.: The Brookings Institution, 1992), p. 148.
11. Manning, *The New Canada*, p.317.
12. *Ibid.*
13. Preston Manning. "A New and Better Home for Canadians," keynote address, Reform Party Assembly, Ottawa, October 15, 1994.
14. Simpson, *Faultlines*, p.123.
15. *The Gallup Poll*, January 10, 1994.
16. The 1992 Constitutional Referendum Study asked respondents to score "immigrants" on a "feeling thermometer" ranging from 0 (very cold, negative) to 100 (very warm, positive). The average score assigned to "immigrants" by Western Canadian respondents was 63.8, which

did not differ significantly from the average of 63.1 for Atlantic respondents and 65.7 for Ontario respondents. Only Quebec respondents, with an average score of 56.2, were significantly different.

17. Alberta has never had a CCF or NDP government, nor for that matter a significant CCF/NDP legislative opposition.

18. February 17, 1960. Cited in smith, *Building a Province*, p. 335.

19. J.F. Conway, *The West: The History of a Region in Confederation* (Toronto: James Lorimer, 1994), p. 330.

20. When the NDP government in Saskatchewan brought in a balanced budget in 1995, Premier Roy Romanow and Finance Minister Janice MacKinnon were quick to contrast their policy with that of neighbouring Alberta. Romanow argued that "Alberta's regime of severe restraint would never fly with a majority of Saskatchewan taxpayers," and MacKinnon noted that "while Alberta opted for deep program cuts, Saskatchewan balanced cuts with tax increases." Both linked the provincial differences to cultural traditions extending back to the Depression. See David Roberts, "Saskatchewan deficit-free one year ahead of schedule," *Globe and Mail*, February 16, 1995.

21. Allyson Jeffs, "Klein tells feds: 'Follow us,'" *Calgary Herald*, January 19, 1995, p. A1.

22. The Gallup Report, June 10, 1992.

23. This construction of the amending formula was of particular importance to the Alberta governments led by Peter Lougheed.

24. J. Peter Meekison, "Alberta and the Constitution," in Allan Tupper and Roger Gibbins, eds., *Government and Politics in Alberta* (Edmonton: University of Alberta Press, 1992), p. 249.

25. Don Braid and Sydney Sharpe, *Breakup: Why the West Feels Left Out of Canada* (Toronto: Key Porter Books, 1990), p. 28.

26. David J. Mitchell, *WAC: Bennett and the Rise of British Columbia* (Vancouver: Douglas & McIntyre, 1983), p. 398.

27. Jeffrey Simpson, "For Mike Harcourt, the sun shines brightly on the New Democrats," *Globe and Mail*, February 17, 1995, p. A18.

28. Braid and Sharpe, *Breakup*, p. 203. Note their use of "regional" rather than "provincial" equality.

29. W.L. Morton, "The Bias of Prairie Politics," *Transactions of the Royal Society of Canada*, series 3, vol. 49, June 1955, p. 66.

30. George Melnyk, *Beyond Alienation: Political Essays on the West* (Calgary: Detselig Press, 1993), p. 119.

31. Rafe Mair, "B.C. Wants Bigger Voice in Ottawa's Spending," *Financial Post*, August 19, 1994, p. 9.

32. Personal correspondence with the authors, June 22, 1994.

33. Gerald Friesen, *The Canadian Prairies: A History* (Toronto: University of Toronto Press, 1994).

34. Allan Kornberg, William Mishler, and Harold D. Clarke, *Representative Democracy in the Canadian Provinces* (Toronto: Prentice-Hall, 1982), p.35.

35. *Ibid.*, p. 38.

36. Cited in R. Gibbins, K. Archer, and S. Drabek, *Canadian Political Life: An Alberta Perspective* (Dubuque, Iowa: Kendall/Hunt, 1990), p. 229.

37. *The Gallup Report*, August 13, 1991.

38. David Laycock, *Populism and Democratic Thought in the Canadian Prairies, 1910-1945* (Toronto: University of Toronto Press, 1990).

39. Sydney Sharpe and Don Braid, *Storming Babylon: Preston Manning and the Rise of the Reform Party* (Toronto: Key Porter Books, 1992), p.61.

40. Immigrants such as William Irvine were important in bringing the American experience into play in the Canadian West, and Preston Manning has been a close student of the American populist experience.

41. Western enthusiasm for recall goes back before the First World War. In 1936, the new Social Credit government in Alberta provided the first legislative enactment of recall in legislation that was then itself "recalled" in 1937 when constituency unrest threatened Premier Aberhart. David Laycock, "Reforming Canadian Democracy? Institutions and Ideology in the Reform Party Project," *Canadian Journal of Political Science*, xxvii: 2 (June 1994), p. 241.

42. For a wide-ranging historical and contemporary discussion of populism and direct democra-

cy, see Patrick Boyer, *Direct Democracy in Canada: The History and Future of Referendums* (Toronto: Dundurn Press, 1992).

43. A recall is a means by which voters can force a sitting member of a legislative assembly to stand for re-election before the end of his or her term. There is no federal provision for recall, but provincial legislation in British Columbia does permit recall elections under tightly constrained conditions.

44. Legislative initiative is a means by which voters can place a proposed piece of legislation on the ballot, and thereby circumvent the legislative assembly. Voters, in effect, can legislate. Here again, there is no federal initiative mechanism, and only British Columbia has formally proposed a process—a very arduous one—by which voters can launch initiatives. However, initiatives are commonly used in the western United States.

45. Mitchell, *WAC*, p. 120.

46. *Ibid.*, p. 236.

47. Simpson, *Faultlines*, p. 121.

48. Manning, *The New Canada*, p. 119.

49. Cited in Margaret Wente, ed., *I Never Say Anything Provocative* (Toronto: Peter Martin, 1975), p.84.

50. The uneasy internal tension between the populist principles of the Reform party and the somewhat autocratic leadership style of Preston Manning has been addressed elsewhere. For example, see Murray Dobbin, *Preston Manning and the Reform Party* (Toronto: James Lorimer, 1991), pp. 211-2. For a useful discussion of left and right populism, see Laycock, "Reforming Canadian Democracy?"

51. Ron Graham, *One-Eyed Kings* (Toronto: Totem, 1986), p. 131.

52. *Calgary Herald*, April 12, 1977, p. 7.

53. Robert Mason Lee, "Parizeau Finds That Presumption, Not Power, Is All That's Needed," *Globe and Mail*, November 19, 1994, p. D2.

54. Dennis Gruending, *Promises to Keep: A Political Biography of Allan Blakeney* (Saskatoon: Western Producer Prairie Books, 1990), p. 190.

55. Barry Cooper, "Looking Eastward, Looking Backward: A Western Reading of the Never-Ending Story," in Curtis Cook, ed., *Constitutional Predicament: Canada after the Referendum of 1992* (Montreal & Kingston: McGill-Queen's University Press, 1994), p. 107. Cooper is more inclined than are most Canadian constitutional scholars to detect a principled foundation to federalism.

56. Joe Clark, *A Nation Too Good To Lose* (Toronto: Key Porter Books, 1994), p. 103.

57. *The Gallup Report*, September 24, 1992.

58. For an extended discussion, see Boyer, *Direct Democracy in Canada*.

59. Legislation now exists in British Columbia for popular legislative initiatives, but the process is daunting in the extreme.

60. André Blais and Elisabeth Gidengil, *Making Representative Democracy Work: The Views of Canadians* (Toronto: Dundurn Press, 1991), p. 19.

61. Simpson, *Faultlines*, p. 117.

62. Tom Flanagan, *Waiting for the Wave: The Reform Party and Preston Manning* (Toronto: Stoddart, 1995), p. 34.

63. Sharpe and Braid, *Storming Babylon*.

64. Reform Party of Canada, *The Blue Book: Principles and Policies* (Calgary: The Reform Party of Canada, 1991), p. 4.

65. Laycock, "Reforming Canadian Democracy?", p. 221.

66. *Ibid.*, p. 243.

67. *Ibid.*, p. 245.

68. *Ibid.*, p. 246.

69. *Ibid.*, p. 214.

70. *Ibid.*, p. 217.

71. David J. Bercuson and Barry Cooper, *Derailed: The Betrayal of the National Dream* (Toronto: Key Porter Books, 1994), p. 201.

72. Braid and Sharpe, *Breakup*, p. 5. On the same page they go on to write: "Most of all, westerners resent having their opinions dismissed as crackpot because they aren't necessarily what Ontario wants to hear."

73. Meekison, "Alberta and the Constitution," p. 254.

# CHAPTER FOUR

# The Quest for a Solution

Western Canadians have long confronted a political system which they believe is stacked against their economic interests, and which fails to reflect their vision of the Canadian federal state. Although the accuracy of this perception is open to debate, its pervasiveness is not; the region's political culture is characterized by a widespread sense of alienation from the national political system. As we concluded in Chapter Two, the basic problem rests not with transient political authorities and the public policy disputes of the moment. Rather, Western Canadians have come to the conclusion that the problem is deeply embedded within the political regime and the nature of Canadian parliamentary government. Perhaps surprisingly, however, alienation has not led to political apathy, disengagement, or withdrawal.[1] Instead, the West has spawned a large number of protest movements, new political parties, and other initiatives all designed to address the root causes of western alienation. It is our intention in this chapter to explore this ongoing quest and to explain why, in the final analysis, generations of political protest have failed to leave any significant mark on Canada's institutional fabric.

The chapter is structured around the distinctions drawn in Chapter Two among the political *authorities*, the political *regime*, and the political *community*. We begin by addressing a number of ways in which Western Canadians have tried to realize their aspirations through changes to the political authorities, and to the public policies associated with those authorities. We then turn to proposed solutions which have been directed more to the nature of the political regime than to transient authorities; these solutions will include nonpartisanship, populism, greater decentralization of the federal state, and Senate reform, solutions which have enjoyed varying levels of support over time and across the four provinces. In conclusion, we will address solutions which challenge the nature of the political community.

Before embarking upon this endeavour, it is important to remember that regional discontent has not been driven exclusively by economic grievances. As we explained in the last chapter, Western Canadians have developed positive visions of the federal state, which are deeply rooted in the values of the regional community. The frustration they have experienced in having these visions accepted as legitimate *national* visions is an important component of western alienation, and thus the "quest for a solution" extends beyond redress for specific instances of public policy discontent. It is also a search for an institutional framework more in tune with regional values and aspirations. Just as Québécois nationalism cannot be seen exclusively as a reaction to the perceived mistreatment of Quebec within Canada, western discontent cannot be seen exclusively as a reaction to perceived mistreatment of the West. At the core of each lie positive visions of the future that draw upon dreams as much as upon anger. The difference is that western dreams have been anchored traditionally to Canada as the essential national community; they have not included an independent West. Whether this difference will persist is a matter to which we return in conclusion.

CHALLENGES TO POLITICAL AUTHORITIES

When David Easton referred to political authorities, he had in mind those individuals who hold formal positions of authority within the political institutions of the country.[2] At the very least, they would include the prime minister and members of the federal cabinet, the provincial premiers, and national party leaders, but the term can also be expanded to include both the political parties which provide a vehicle for leadership and the various policies associated with the authorities of the day. Taken together, these elements encompass many of the targets of western alienation. It is not surprising, then, that Western Canadians have often sought the solution to their discontent through a change in the composition of political authorities. At times, however, they have pursued changes in the fabric of public policy as a source of broader leverage on regional discontent.

*The policy challenge*

As we saw in Chapter Two, Western Canadians can recall a litany of national policies that have worked to the disadvantage of the region. This part of the regional political culture is learned early and rarely forgotten. Indeed, it is so accessible and so easily learned that newcomers to the region can drape themselves with the mantle of western alienation after spending only a few months in the West. In most respects, these policies are seen as symptomatic of more deep-seated structural and institutional inequities; "the problem" is thought to lie elsewhere, and thus must be addressed through changes to political actors or institutions. There comes to mind, however, one policy issue of much broader significance: the implementation of free trade has been seen by many Westerners as part of the solution to a much larger problem relating to the nature of political power in Canada.

For most of the twentieth century, Prairie residents argued that the national tariff policy worked to the disadvantage of the West. As Steve Dorey explains, "the west has traditionally viewed protection in Canada as a device designed to transfer wealth generated by world-class resource exporters competing freely in world markets to eastern manufacturers who had neither the ability nor the inclination to compete in open international markets."[3] Free trade was therefore promoted as a way to end the regional inequities of the tariff system by enabling prairie farmers to compete on an equal footing in the international marketplace with American agricultural producers. However, when the Mulroney government began to promote free trade with the United States, "a diversity of expectations and concerns" came to the fore.[4] As the free trade debate unfolded, it became clear that the region's historical consensus on the virtues of free trade did not extend to the Free Trade Agreement (FTA) with the United Sates or to the North American Free Trade Agreement (NAFTA) with the United States and Mexico.

When free trade was packaged in the late 1980s as the proposed FTA, it was sold to Western Canadians as an economic and *political* package. In an extraordinary 1988 speech to the Calgary Petroleum Club, federal energy minister Pat Carney argued that the FTA would provide a means of political protection for Western Canadians *from their own national government*! If, she said, Ottawa was tempted in the future to impose another National Energy Program, this would be prohibited under the terms of the FTA. In effect, Carney stated, Washington would come to the region's defence if it were to be faced again by a predatory Canadian government. The more general point is that free trade, as embodied in both the FTA and NAFTA, promised to tie the hands of national governments with respect to economic management. Given that Ottawa's economic management has traditionally been a source of concern rather than comfort for Western Canadians, it is not surprising that free trade was supported by many for both economic and political reasons. If Western Canadians could not convince the national government to serve regional interests better, they could at least shackle that government so that it would be less able to act against those interests.[5]

However, it was this very potential to shackle the federal government that opened up intraregional fissures in the free trade debate. As discussed in Chapter Three, there are Western Canadian visions that are dependent upon a strong national government, and therefore the potential of free trade agreements to erode the capacity of governments, both federal and provincial, to support economic and social development programs was viewed with considerable alarm in parts of the West. When it is also recognized that the petroleum industry was a clear winner in the agreement, and that short-term benefits to the agricultural sector were relatively minor,[6] it is not surprising that significant provincial differences emerged with respect to support for the agreement. Figure 4.1 shows that in three of the four western provinces, a clear majority of respondents to the 1991 Angus Reid survey felt that the FTA had hurt their province, at least in the short run. Indeed, only among Albertans do we find some modestly positive perceptions of the FTA, and even here the

FIGURE 4.1    Perceived Effect of Free Trade Agreement

"The Canada-U.S. Free Trade Agreement has now been in effect for two years. Generally speaking, would you say that, so far, having the free trade agreement with the United States has benefited your province, hurt your province, or hasn't really had any impact one way or the other yet?"

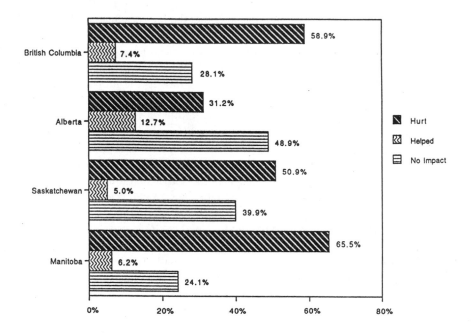

*Source*: Options for Western Canada Study, 1991

**Table 4.1**

Pro-FTA Vote in the 1988 Election

|  | Man | Sask | Alberta | B.C. |
|---|---|---|---|---|
| % voting Conservative | 36.9 | 36.4 | 51.8 | 34.4 |
| % voting Reform | 5.3 | 1.2 | 17.1 | 7.3 |
| Total pro-FTA vote | 42.2% | 37.6% | 68.9% | 41.7% |

number of respondents concluding that the FTA had hurt the province out-numbered those who felt that it had helped it by a margin of more than two to one. When respondents were asked whether they thought the FTA would help or hurt their province over the longer term, they were more likely to perceive benefits; 40.3 per cent of the Alberta respondents, 27.2 per cent of British Columbia respondents, 25.7 per cent of Saskatchewan respondents, and 25.6 per cent of those from Manitoba expected their province to benefit over the next ten to fifteen years. However, more respondents anticipated long-term hurt, and only in Alberta did those expecting benefits outnumber those expecting their province to be hurt.[7]

Provincial differences with respect to the FTA were also manifest in the 1988 election results. In the 1988 campaign, which in many ways boiled down to a national referendum on free trade, the Progressive Conservatives and Reform supported the proposed FTA while the Liberals and New Democrats opposed it. As Table 4.1 shows, the total pro-FTA vote was much higher in Alberta than it was elsewhere in the West. Indeed, in the other three provinces the parties opposed to the FTA captured a clear majority of the popular vote.

It is ironic that the Conservative government, in moving to address a long-standing Western Canadian preference for free trade, should have encountered such strong regional opposition. Perhaps the explanation comes in part from the feeling that Ottawa acted too late. Note, for example, Preston Manning's interpretation of the Mulroney initiative: "Even the FTA was sort of a concession. The West had been screaming for free trade since the days of the CPR, but Mulroney and those guys didn't hear until Quebec wanted free trade."[8] There is also no question that the nature of the regional and international economies had changed dramatically from the early period of agrarian settlement, and that the national tariff system had already been reduced to near insignificance by the evolution of the General Agreement on Tariffs and Trade (GATT). By the late 1980s free trade had come to be viewed with trepidation by western agricultural producers who saw very minor tariff relief coupled with the rapid erosion of national programs designed to offer some protection from the vagaries of the international market.

When viewed from an historical perspective, the free trade issue stands apart from other policy disputes. It was used by Western Canadians to illustrate how the Canadian economy and, more importantly, national economic policy discriminated against regional interests. How parties stood with respect to the free trade issue was often used as the litmus test for regional fairness. Yet, by the time of the FTA, free trade had lost its ability to unite the region. Indeed, and with the possible exception of Albertans, Western Canadians were opposed to the free trade initiatives of the Mulroney government. Thus if regional concerns and aspirations were to be addressed, they would have to be addressed through some strategy other than the adoption of free trade.

*Playing the major party game*

Conventional democratic politics offers a ready means to express regional discontent and to pursue regional interests. Quite simply, one can hope to capture the government of the day and infuse that government with regional actors, perspectives, aspirations, and visions. If this fails, if the government remains wedded to opposing regional interests or national visions, then voters can throw their support behind the primary opposition party in the hope that it will form the government and thus redress regional grievances. In short, a region can try to protect its interests by offering electoral support in exchange for favourable policy treatment. If this reciprocal agreement is broken, then the regional electorate can attempt to "throw the bastards out" and vote in new bastards with a more favourable disposition. Western Canadians have long played this game, although they have seldom won.

The political history of the West, and particularly the prairie West, has been characterized by sustained periods of support for first one and then the other of the two major parties that have until recently dominated the national landscape. Throughout most of the first sixty years of the twentieth century, the federal Liberals easily out-polled the Conservatives on the Prairies. In federal elections held from 1900 to 1957 inclusive, the Liberals won 263 prairie seats compared to only 141 for the Conservatives, for a margin of almost two to one. (In British Columbia, however, the Conservatives won 90 federal seats over the same period, compared to 67 for the Liberals, an outcome that once again demonstrates the distinctive history of British Columbia.) This was a time when the Conservatives were closely associated with the National Policy and its tariffs, and with economic interests based in Ontario. It was also a time of considerable Liberal success as the party was in power for 41 of the 57 years. The region, therefore, was onside with the government of the day for most of the period.

However, the apparent conclusion drawn by Western Canadians was that being part of the governing coalition was not all that advantageous if the coalition's centre of gravity was to be found outside the region. The Liberals' leadership during this period—Wilfrid Laurier, Mackenzie King, Louis St. Laurent—came from outside the region, and the party's electoral heartland was to be found in Quebec, not in the West. In the elections from 1900 to 1957 inclusive, the Liberals won 853 seats in Quebec compared to 330 across the four western provinces, for a Quebec-to-West ratio of 2.6 to 1. (During this time period, Quebec's population was also slightly larger: on average, 28.5% of the national population lived in Quebec compared to 24.6% in Western Canada.)

Fidelity to the Liberal party was therefore not seen as the sole solution, and it was during this time, particularly from 1921 on, that western voters turned to a variety of third parties. Indeed, in total there were more CCF, Progressive, Social Credit and independent MPs elected across the region than there were Liberals: 348 were elected compared to the 330 Liberal MPs in the period stretching from 1900 to 1957. If we look only at the period from 1921 on, when the first regional party burst upon the scene, third party MPs from Western Canada outnumbered Liberal MPs by a margin of 348 to 261.

In the 1958 election, voters gave John Diefenbaker's Progressive Conservatives the largest victory ever recorded in Canada when the Tories took 208 of the 265 seats in the House, compared to only 49 for the Liberals. The landslide included all but 5 of the 70 seats in Western Canada, and sounded the death knell for the national wings of the western-based CCF and Social Credit. (The former nonetheless won the 1960 provincial election in Saskatchewan, and the latter survived as a provincial force in Alberta into the late 1970s and in British Columbia into the early 1990s.) What set the West apart was not the regional success of the Conservatives in 1958, for they were successful everywhere, including Quebec, but rather that Western Canadians stayed in the Conservative camp long after voters elsewhere had drifted back to the Liberal fold. In the eight federal elections held between 1962 and 1980, inclusive, the Conservatives won 291 seats on the Prairies compared to only 28 for the Liberals. In British Columbia, the Conservatives won 69 seats compared to 47 for the Liberals. Thus during a time of sustained Liberal hegemony in Ottawa, the West remained lodged firmly, even stubbornly, in the camp of the official Opposition.

Then, when western loyalty finally paid off in 1984 as the Mulroney Conservatives swept to power,[9] the reaction in the West was one of rapid disappointment. As explained in Chapter Two, Western Canadians appear to have focused their attention on the policy miscues of the Conservative government rather than upon the significant steps it took to address regional concerns. The CF-18 dispute, for example, "confirmed to Preston Manning's satisfaction that a rotation of parties in Ottawa did not bring fundamental change, since both were driven by the political exigencies of Old Canada."[10] Moreover, the Conservative success in 1984 was not due to western support; it came about because the party captured a huge majority of the Ontario and Quebec seats.

In fact, the Conservatives would have formed a majority government in 1984 even if they had failed to win a single seat in Western Canada. The West, therefore, was not the linchpin of Conservative success, but a frill.

It might be expected that discontent with the party system would have prompted Western Canadian interest in electoral reform as a means to increase regional leverage. During the 1970s and early 1980s, the Liberals were able to form a series of minority and majority governments without winning a significant number of seats in Western Canada, and without winning any in Alberta. The best and most troubling example of this came in 1980, when the newly elected Liberal majority included only two Western Canadian MPs, both from Manitoba. The Liberals' failure to win seats in the West was in part a result of the single-member, first-past-the-post electoral system. They did reasonably well in terms of the popular vote, often winning between 25 and 30 per cent of the regional vote, but these votes were not translated into an equivalent number of seats in the House of Commons. For instance, in 1980, when the Liberals won only two of the 77 seats in Western Canada, they still picked up 23 per cent of the regional popular vote. Hence, there was an argument to be made that the country would be better served by the adoption of some form of proportional representation which would ensure that no region was shut out of national power as the West had been, and as Quebec briefly was following the Conservative win in 1979. Proposals for reform ranged from complete systems of proportional representation to more complicated compromises whereby seats won in the conventional manner would be "topped up" by a limited number of MPs elected by proportional representation formulae.

Electoral reform, however, did not catch on as a popular solution to the representation problems facing the West even though the region had some past experience with electoral innovation. The Saskatchewan Progressive Association had proposed the adoption of the single transferable vote in 1930,[11] both Manitoba and Alberta had experimented with proportional representation, and British Columbia had briefly adopted the single transferrable ballot, although all such innovations had been abandoned by the late 1950s. More recently, the 1991 Angus Reid survey showed that Western Canadians were still not happy with the electoral status quo. When respondents were asked if the federal electoral system was "effective or not effective in terms of the representation it provides for your province in the federal government," 58.3 per cent said that it was not effective while only 35.4 per cent said it was. Discontent was expressed across the region, with the proportion saying that the system was not effective ranging only from a low of 51.9 per cent in Saskatchewan to a high of 60.3 per cent in Alberta. Yet although electoral reform found some support among academics,[12] regional think-tanks such as the Canada West Foundation, and the "chattering classes" in general, it never mobilized substantial public support. Moreover, it was rejected by the dominant opposition party in the West, the Progressive Conservatives, who argued there was an easier solution to western discontent: simply elect a Conservative government. This argument was an effective counter to the proponents of electoral reform, although ironically it was later to lend support to the proponents of institutional reform who emerged in the wake of regional discontent with the Mulroney government.

In summary, the Western Canadian conclusion has been that neither alternating regional support between the two major parties, nor remaining faithful to one, is a foolproof or even reasonably effective strategy for the advancement of regional interests and visions. At the same time, electoral reform has not caught on as a solution. As a consequence, there has been a long history of regional support for third parties.

*Creating new parties*

The West has given birth to a number of third parties which, while not formed exclusively to address regional concerns and aspirations, have nonetheless served as important political vehicles for both. These parties have generated a rich and voluminous literature, one that cannot be summarized here.[13] However, it is important for our general thesis to review the highlights of this third party history, and to note the frustrations that it has induced.

The first of the western-based parties to contest a general election, and in some respects the prototype for the contemporary Reform party, was the Progressive Party of Canada. The Progressives emerged in the partisan confusion that followed the end of the First World War, and in the 1921 general election 64 Progressive MPs were elected, compared to 116 Liberals and only 50 Conservatives.[14] Progressive candidates won 37 of the 43 prairie seats and two of 13 seats in British Columbia; they also captured 24 seats in Ontario. Although the Progressives were a regional party in that the majority of Progressive MPs came from the Prairie provinces, the discontent that created and energized the party can best be described as agrarian rather than regional in character. To be sure, the agrarian heartland at the time was to be found in the prairie West, but there was still a large rural community in Ontario which yielded Progressive seats. The agrarian rather than regional nature of the party limited its success in British Columbia and urban Ontario while, ironically, its regional character pre-empted any appeal in the rural parts of Quebec or the Maritime provinces. The Progressives also provided a vehicle for post-war social reformers, and particularly for those associated with the social gospel movement.[15]

There is no question that the Progressives rocked the Canadian party system. Indeed, the two-party system that had been in place since Confederation was never fully restored. However, there is also no question that they failed to leave much of a mark on national public policy. Progressive MPs were uneasy and ineffective within the intensely partisan parliamentary environment. Those from Manitoba and Saskatchewan were largely disenchanted Liberals who were quite willing to return to the Liberal fold if given even modest encouragement to do so, while other Progressive MPs were unwilling to adapt to the partisan conventions of Parliament. As a consequence, the loosely-knit Progressives allowed the smaller Conservative caucus to form the official Opposition, and many Progressive MPs, including their leader, T.A. Crerar, soon fell prey to the personal and policy inducements offered by Liberal prime minister Mackenzie King, who adopted large portions of the Progressives' tariff and social policy. (King cleverly described the Progressive MPs as "Liberals in a hurry," a description that facilitated their absorption by his own party.) By the 1925 election the Liberals were rebuilding traditional areas of strength in Manitoba and Saskatchewan, and the Progressives were in full retreat; only 24 MPs were elected, and of those only two came from Ontario and none from British Columbia. A year later, 20 were elected, including two from Ontario and 11 from Alberta. By the 1930 election, the Progressives were reduced to a small Alberta enclave, with 9 of their 12 MPs elected from that province. The party evaporated soon after, with the remnants of the Progressive movement being absorbed by the nascent CCF and Social Credit parties. The Progressive mixture of agrarian, regional, and social discontent was an explosive force in 1921, but it failed to promote any lasting reform of the political regime. It provided dramatic expression of regional discontent with conventional party politics and the partisan constraints in Parliament, but it failed to replace either one. If anything, the Progressives demonstrated the inability of a western-based party, even one with reasonable initial representation from Ontario, to significantly alter the political landscape in Ottawa.

The dilemma for any western-based party has been to find a way to expand beyond the region without losing the regional support that led to its formation in the first place. If the party remains bottled up within the region, then there is no prospect of forming the national government, for there are not enough seats in Western Canada. Given that the conventions of parliamentary government provide little effective leverage for opposition parties or individual MPs, to remain a regional party is to be resigned to political impotence. Here a good example is provided by Social Credit, which had quite remarkable provincial success in Alberta and British Columbia. In the former case, Social Credit had an unbroken hold on office from 1935 to 1971. Ernest Manning served as premier for 25 years, and delivered an unflamboyant style of conservative, frugal, and honest government that left his party's provincial hegemony virtually unchallenged. In British Columbia, Social Credit dominated provincial politics from the early 1950s to the late 1980s with a dramatically different but equally successful style of government. Yet the *national* Social Credit party was unable to use its provincial beachheads for an effective assault on federal office. Admittedly, it did enjoy substantial success in Alberta from 1935 to 1958: the party captured over 60 per cent of the seats across the seven elections, although it averaged only 35 per cent of the popular vote. (Of all Social

Credit MPs elected over this period, 86% came from Alberta.) However, the national party made very limited inroads in British Columbia, electing only 17 MPs in the six elections held between 1953 and 1965. The Alberta Social Credit MPs left no positive mark in Ottawa, and served primarily to isolate the province from the national mainstream; they were an object of caricature and amusement rather than a means of effective regional representation. The lesson, then, is that there is a need to expand beyond regional boundaries, to appeal at least to the Ontario electorate, but to do so in a way that does not neglect regional concerns. This is not an easy balance to maintain, and whether the Reform party will be able to pull it off remains to be seen.[16]

A second western-based party to emerge in the 1930s was the Co-operative Commonwealth Federation (CCF), founded at meetings in Calgary (1932) and Regina (1933). Within the context of the Great Depression and its particularly harsh impact on the Prairies, the CCF brought together the remnants of the Progressives, the United Farmers of Alberta, a collection of small socialist parties, the Brotherhood of Railway Employees, and the League for Social Reconstruction, an eastern-based group of intellectuals moulded along the lines of the British Fabian Society. The heterogeneous nature of the new party was reflected in its full name: the Co-operative Commonwealth Federation (Farmer, Labour, Socialist). In principle, the CCF was anything but a regional party; its founding documents stressed the need for national economic planning and gave short shrift to both provincial governments and the need for regional representation within parliamentary institutions. Regional conflict was acknowledged, but only as a symptom of "the inherent contradictions of capitalism."[17] Yet in practice, the CCF was lodged emphatically in the West, and even more so in Saskatchewan where it first won provincial office in 1944. Of the party's 112 MPs elected from 1935 to 1958, 63 per cent came from the Prairie provinces, 46 per cent came from Saskatchewan alone, and 26 per cent coming from British Columbia; only 12 MPs were elected from outside the region over the seven general elections.[18] The leadership of the party—J.S. Woodsworth, M.J. Coldwell, T.C. (Tommy) Douglas, and Stanley Knowles—came from the West and gave the CCF an indelible regional stamp that limited its electoral appeal outside the region. Thus, although the CCF set out to transcend regionalism in the quest for fundamental changes to the economic system, it became one of a series of western-based parties operating at the margins of Parliament.

In the wake of Diefenbaker's sweep in 1958, which reduced the CCF to only 8 seats in the House of Commons, the CCF was folded into the New Democratic Party. The founding convention of the NDP in 1960 brought together the remains of the CCF with the Canadian Labour Congress and urban social democrats. There was, understandably, a desire among the founders of the NDP to escape the regional limitations of the CCF, and in this respect the new party was reasonably successful. Although there was still a western stamp to the party, one underscored by the selection of

Saskatchewan's Tommy Douglas as the party's new leader, and although its provincial successes came largely in the West, the NDP was able to achieve a national profile of sorts. In practice, this meant reasonable success in Ontario, for the NDP, like the CCF before it, made no headway in Quebec and very little headway in Atlantic Canada. Still, in the final analysis, the party's seats in the House of Commons came predominantly from the West. Of the 264 NDP MPs elected from 1962 through 1993, 66 per cent came from the four western provinces, 37 per cent came from British Columbia alone, and only 30 per cent came from Ontario. The NDP's share of the popular vote showed a more national distribution of support, but the operation of the electoral system pinned the party's centre of gravity to the West.

What, then, do we conclude from this brief history? Western Canadians have been instrumental in establishing a series of third parties that have enjoyed strong support within the region, and have been significant if somewhat idiosyncratic players on the national stage. However, none of these parties has come even close to achieving national office; any parliamentary leverage they have found has come during times of Liberal minority governments. True, in the 1993 election Reform came within two seats of forming the Official Opposition, a prize captured by the Bloc Québécois, and western parties including Reform have effectively destroyed the two-party system in Canada, but legislative *power* has remained elusive. Thus as *vehicles of regional discontent* they can best be seen as symptomatic of the problems Western Canadians have faced within the national political process rather than as an effective response to those problems. What remains to be seen is whether the Reform party can break the mould for parties originating in Western Canada. When Reform was founded in 1987, its primary concern was for more effective representation for the West within the national government. To date, the Reform's success has been overwhelmingly in the West, with only a single Reform MP having been elected outside the region. At the same time, Reform has been moving steadily away from regional themes to address issues of more national appeal such as deficit reduction, tax reform, immigration, gun control (or the lack thereof), young offenders and, with increasing hesitation, the appropriate place of Quebec within the Canadian federal state. The next election should determine whether Reform can retain its western base while still winning enough seats outside the region to have a shot at national office. History suggests that the odds of success are not good.

CHALLENGES TO THE POLITICAL REGIME

Regional frustration with traditional forms of party politics, and with the inability of regional third parties to achieve significant parliamentary leverage, has led Western Canadians to question the institutional status quo. Challenges to the political regime have ranged from the rejection of the partisan underpinnings of national politics to proposals for new institutional arrangements that would better provide for the effective representation of regional interests and aspirations.

## *The rejection of partisanship*

The failure to find a major party champion for regional interests and visions, and the failure to date of third parties to achieve effective policy leverage, has led to an understandable regional disenchantment with partisanship. Despite this, the Western Canadian rejection of partisanship has been far from absolute. Throughout this century, the Conservative and Liberal parties have had a significant regional presence. Even in the dog days of the 1930s and 1940s, when both the CCF and Social Credit were in their prime, Conservative and Liberal candidates on the Prairies still captured between 50 and 60 per cent of the popular vote. When the Progressives swept the Prairies in 1921, the two traditional parties won almost 40 per cent of the popular vote. Moreover, some of the relatively successful third parties in the West have been very partisan creatures; neither the CCF nor the NDP was nonpartisan in any sense of the term. Nonetheless, there has been an important regional current of "nonpartisanship" that has taken two different, albeit related, forms. The first challenged partisanship directly; the second has come to find expression within the broader ideological vehicle of populism.

The frustrations that Western Canadians have encountered with partisan constraints in the House of Commons, and with national parties preoccupied with the interests of the Central Canadian electorate, have led to a significant and durable regional interest in nonpartisanship. What would happen, Westerners have asked, if candidates ran without party labels and were responsible only to their local constituents? Would MPs then be able to speak more openly and effectively on behalf of their constituents, and would this result in more effective regional representation? At the very least, could the partisan constraints on MPs be relaxed under some conditions so that regional interests were not routinely subordinated to those of party?

There was considerable interest in nonpartisanship in the early decades of prairie settlement, particularly in Alberta. As C. B. Macpherson has argued, both the United Farmers of Alberta and Social Credit represented an attack on the partisan organization of political life:

> the radicalism of both movements consisted not so much in the extent of their economic demands (which were not extreme) as in their conviction, born of repeated frustration of those demands, that the economic subordination from which they were suffering was an inherent part of eastern financial domination and the party system.[19]

The Nonpartisan League, which had originated in the United States, and the United Farmers of Manitoba attracted a good deal of support with their vision of legislative assemblies freed from partisan constraints. The underlying principle of nonpartisanship, which gave primacy to the interests of local constituents and thereby forged a closer bond between the elected representative and the community which he or she represented, was of considerable appeal in a region where voters felt their MPs soon lost touch with western concerns. The supporters of nonpartisanship also assumed that the power of financial interests could be curtailed through nonpartisanship, as it would not be necessary for candidates to raise large sums of money to fight a national or provincial campaign.

Unfortunately, unadulterated nonpartisanship would not make much sense as an organizing principle for Parliament, and the critics of partisanship have been slow to propose workable alternatives.[20] Although nonpartisanship may have some applicability within the context of local or even provincial government, it could not provide any effective orchestration of the national legislature. Close to 300 independent MPs cannot *govern*, or at least cannot do so in a coherent fashion. Parliamentary democracy requires a government, and modern governments are held together by the glue of partisanship which provides cabinet stability, allows a prime minister to be selected, structures parliamentary debate, and facilitates responsible government by making it clear to voters who is to blame for the action or inaction of the day. A voter who could pass judgment only on his or her local MP, and who could not reward or punish the *government*, would be stripped of any effective power. Partisanship may constrain the freedom of MPs, but it empowers the electorate. All this, however, is not to say that a somewhat more relaxed partisan environment would be incompatible with responsible parliamentary government. In the United Kingdom, for example, methods have been found to reduce the degree of partisan constraints across a substantial range of legislation.[21] Yet even in this respect, Western Canadian arguments have not taken hold; three decades of parliamentary reform have made virtually no impact on the pervasiveness and centrality of party discipline.

It is worth noting that support for nonpartisanship in the federal arena has not been coupled with any uniform regional support for it in the provincial arena. The strongest support for provincial nonpartisanship, or at least for the spirit thereof, has been found in Alberta, where provincial governments, backed by large legislative majorities, have often taken on a nonpartisan veneer. Alberta premiers have been comfortable with a leadership style analogous to that of a chairman of the board, someone who presides over a relatively homogeneous electorate and sees partisan conflict as indicative of poor manners and a lack of taste. Provincial premiers act as if they are "above all that." In Manitoba, the victory of the United Farmers in the early 1920s ushered in a period of nonpartisan government that lasted until the provincial Conservatives took office in 1958. Although the underlying reality of nonpartisanship in Manitoba has been questioned,[22] and although the Manitoba experience was based on a municipal model rather than on the ideological rejection of partisanship which was more characteristic of the Alberta experience, nonpartisanship has still been an important feature of the provincial political culture. Saskatchewan, however, "has always enjoyed, in every sense of the term, partisan politics."[23] The intense two-party competition between first, the CCF and the Liberals, and second, the NDP and the Conservatives, was very ideological in character, and left no room for nonpartisan cooperation. Virtually the same conclusion holds for British Columbia, where a "no holds barred, no prisoners taken" style of partisan and ideological combat has characterized the political culture for generations. Certainly no premier in British Columbia can assume that he or she speaks for the entire provincial electorate, an assumption made routinely by premiers in Alberta.

Of course, the lack of support for nonpartisanship in the provincial arena does not rule it out as a regional strategy in the federal Parliament. However, it does suggest that the tenets of nonpartisanship may not be deeply embedded in the regional political culture, and that nonpartisanship constitutes a strategic rather than principled response to the representational problems lying at the root of western alienation. Given the practical problems of nonpartisanship, it is not surprising that its advocates failed to make much headway. Much as people disliked the constraints of party discipline in the House, nonpartisanship by itself did not appear to offer a viable alternative. At least, it failed to do so until the populist advocacy of direct democracy offered a means by which citizens could circumvent the highly partisan institutions of representative democracy.

## Populism revisited

As we discussed in Chapter Three, the general tenets of populism fit neatly within the Western Canadian political culture. The belief that external elites are dominating national politics, that representative institutions fail to provide adequate protection for regional interests, and that individuals should carry equal weight within the political process are all staples of the regional political culture, and all imply support for populist alternatives. Yet despite the fact that some populist initiatives date back to the turn of the century,[24] the West has been slow to embrace populist approaches to government. The tenets of populism have shaped perceptions of the political world, but its institutional prescriptions have been slow to win more than tentative public approval.

The early roots of populism are to be found in the support for nonpartisanship discussed above, and in some of the early initiatives of the Social Credit movement. It was Alberta Social Credit, for example, that first enacted legislation permitting constituents to recall sitting members of the provincial legislature, legislation that was repealed shortly after it was introduced when Premier Aberhart's constituents in Okotoks-High River threatened to bring it into play. Then, for most of the next fifty years, there were few new initiatives. To be sure, elite bashing played a significant role in electoral politics, particularly when those elites could be placed outside the region, but this was little more than run-of-the-mill democratic politics. Western Canadians protested the results of representative democracy, but did not successfully advance ways in which elected representatives could be circumvented or more effectively brought into line with constituency opinion.

This situation changed significantly with the emergence of Reform, and with developments in national constitutional politics. Reform was the first western-based party to wholeheartedly endorse populist principles, and to propose a series of procedures through which the "common sense of the common people" could be given an effective voice. Reform advocates not only the recall of sitting members who are out of line with constituency opinion, but also the use of referendums and initiatives to provide direct legislative input. As the opening passage of the party's 1993 Blue Book states, "We believe in the common sense of the common people, their right to be consulted on public policy matters before major decisions are made, their right to choose and recall their own representatives and to govern themselves through truly representative and responsible institutions, and their right to directly initiate legislation for which substantial public support is demonstrated." Within the party itself, there has been enthusiastic support for town-hall meetings, both traditional and electronic, and for the use of polls, voice-mail survey techniques, and the Internet, through which constituents can register their opinions on the controversies of the day. In many ways, therefore, Reform's platform constitutes a broad attack on, and an alternative to, conventional forms of representative democracy.

Yet despite the energy and enthusiasm that Reform has pumped into populist techniques, it is doubtful whether there would have been a significant public response had it not been for developments on the constitutional front. The constitutional amending formula adopted in 1982, which required legislative consent for future amendments and therefore opened the door to public hearings, as well as the anguished national debates over the Meech Lake and Charlottetown Accords, in which an elite consensus slowly dissolved before an increasingly estranged citizenry, all provided impetus for populism. Both Meech and Charlottetown gave clear evidence that on matters of fundamental principle, representative elites were out of touch with those whom they were presumably representing. Additional impetus for populism came from the imposition of the GST despite overwhelming public opposition. Therefore we have witnessed growing public and even governmental enthusiasm for the techniques of direct democracy, enthusiasm that may be more pronounced in the West than it is elsewhere because of the more supportive regional political culture. We see, then, the requirements in Alberta and British Columbia that constitutional amendments be put to the people before they receive legislative consent, legislation in British Columbia that permits citizen initiatives and the recall of sitting MLAs, and legislation in Manitoba and Alberta that would require future governments to go to the people in a referendum before tax increases could be implemented. To all of this we would add the strong support that the Reform party, and presumably its populist stance, received in at least the western half of the region in the 1993 federal election.

Chapter Three provided some empirical evidence of regional support for populism, and the 1992 constitutional referendum survey provides some additional insight. Respondents were asked which is more important in a democratic society: ensuring that the majority decides, or protecting minorities. Among Western Canadian respondents, 58.0 per cent opted for the former and more populist response, with only 29.5 per cent opting for minority protection. Yet, while this may indicate a supportive environment for populism, it is by no means one restricted to the West. In Ontario, 60.8 per cent of respondents chose majority rule, as did 54.3 per cent of those in Atlantic Canada. Only in Quebec did a plurality of respondents (44.5%) choose protecting minorities, with 42.1 per cent choosing majority rule.

In summary, populism is deeply rooted within the regional political culture and enjoys substantial public support. None of this, however, ensures that populist options would provide a more effective voice for regional interests within national institutions. As we noted before, there is an inherent problem for Westerners in relying upon populist techniques when less than 30 per cent of the national population lives in the region. Even if the national government came to rely less heavily on representative democracy and more heavily on populist techniques—a change of emphasis for which there is no evidence in the current Liberal government led by Jean Chrétien—this in itself would not ensure that national policy was any more reflective of western interests, aspirations, and visions. Populism alone provides an incomplete and perhaps even risky solution to the root cause of western alienation. It may not be enough to circumvent representative institutions; those institutions themselves and the federal arrangements within which they are embedded may have to be reformed.

Populism seeks to provide "the people" with more effective leverage on public policy and elected representatives. However, there are aspects of the Canadian state for which populism provides limited leverage, or which seem outside the conventional ambit of populist thought. One of these is the federal division of powers, and a second is the thorny issue of Senate reform.

## Devolution

Federal states provide an important form of protection for regional interests through the constitutional division of powers between the national and provincial governments. The potentially adverse impact of the national government is confined to its own area of legislative competence, and in most cases it cannot infringe upon the legislative sphere of the provinces.[25] It would seem, then, that one strategy to deal with an unsympathetic or hostile national government is to change the constitution in order to constrict the legislative sphere of the national government and expand that of the provincial governments. Decentralization in this form has been the basic constitutional strategy of the Quebec government since at least the onset of the Quiet Revolution in 1960, a strategy that finds its logical extension in contemporary support for sovereignty-association and/or independence. Not surprisingly, decentralization has also been pursued with considerable enthusiasm in recent years by some western provincial governments.

Decentralization would allow western provincial governments to ride on the constitutional coattails of the Quebec government as the latter pushes for, at the very least, a radically decentralized federal state. To some, such as Joe Clark, decentralization offers a context within which Western Canadians might be prepared to accept some form of special status for Quebec.[26] More generally, decentralization has appealed to provincial elites determined to maximize their own jurisdictional control. In the words of Robert Bonner, British Columbia's Attorney General during the premiership of W.A.C. Bennett, "Just stay out of our way and we'll run our own show."[27] Thus we find that in the 1970s and early 1980s there was a degree of convergence between the constitutional objectives of parts of the West and Quebec. Both sought to diminish the role and impact of the federal government, although Quebec sought this to a much greater extent.

Recent surveys provide considerable evidence of public support for greater decentralization. In the 1991 Angus Reid survey, respondents were asked which of three alternatives they would prefer if the constitution were to be redrafted: a substantial reduction in federal powers with these given to all the provinces, the same arrangement between the provinces and the federal government that exists today, or a substantial increase in federal powers with these taken from the provinces. Across the region, 49.5 per cent chose substantial decentralization, 31.8 per cent the status quo, and 13.0 per cent greater centralization. Support for greater decentralization was only somewhat greater in British Columbia and Alberta (49.9% and 54.9% respectively) than it was in Saskatchewan and Manitoba (44.1% and 43.4% respectively). It is interesting to note, however, that respondents by a margin of more than two to one supported "national standards" in program areas controlled by provincial governments. A Gallup survey conducted in May 1992 showed that Western Canadians were more supportive of decentralization than were other Canadians outside Quebec, although the differences were not massive. Respondents were asked the following question: "As a result of the present constitutional discussions, in general would you prefer to see the federal government receive additional powers, would you prefer to see the provincial governments receive additional powers, or would you prefer to maintain the present distribution of powers between the federal and provincial governments?" Greater provincial powers was the option chosen by 35 per cent of Atlantic respondents, 49 per cent of those from Quebec, 31 per cent of those

Public Support for Decentralization

The 1992 constitutional referendum survey asked respondents which government best looked after their needs: the government of Canada, their provincial government, both, or neither. Western Canadian respondents were the most likely to choose provincial governments and, along with Quebec respondents, were the least likely to choose the government of Canada. Although this question does not directly tap constitutional preferences for a more decentralized or centralized federal system, it taps a closely related sentiment.

"Which Government Best Looks After Your Needs?"

|          | Canada | Provincial | Both | Neither |
|----------|--------|------------|------|---------|
| Atlantic | 32.0%  | 45.7       | 8.5  | 10.6    |
| Quebec   | 15.7   | 39.8       | 17.7 | 21.2    |
| Ontario  | 28.0   | 42.4       | 8.0  | 18.8    |
| West     | 16.9   | 52.9       | 11.2 | 14.4    |
|          |        |            |      |         |
| Canada   | 21.8   | 45.1       | 11.5 | 17.5    |

Interestingly, there was virtually no difference in sentiment among the four western provinces. The proportion choosing their provincial government ranged only from a low of 52.4% in British Columbia to a high of 54.8% in Manitoba.

from Ontario, 42 per cent of those on the Prairies, and 45 per cent of those from British Columbia.[28]

Therefore, both governmental and public support have been present for decentralization as an institutional response to western alienation. However, such support has been constrained in the past by the awkward position that Western Canadians found themselves in with respect to the federal system. Although they felt disadvantaged within parliamentary institutions, it was difficult to neutralize those institutions through increased decentralization. The problem was that many of the legislative powers of particular concern to the West were those dealing with interprovincial and international trade. The powers that counted were those relating to such things as tariffs, freight rates, interprovincial railroads and pipelines, national interest rate policy, foreign ownership and investment regulations, corporate tax policy, agricultural marketing and supports, and the promotion of international trade. The dilemma was that these were all powers which adhere intrinsically to the national government in federal states; to assign them to the provinces would be to weaken and perhaps destroy the economic union upon which the political superstructure of the federal state is built. Thus the promotion of a more decentralized federal system faced important logical and structural constraints in the West, constraints that Quebec has not faced so long as the discussion of decentralization focused on legislative powers relating to language, culture, and social programs, all areas of immediate concern to the Quebec National Assembly. To put this conclusion in different words, a concerted push for decentralization by the West could have a more destructive impact on the integrative bonds of Canadian federalism than would such a push by Quebec, provided of course that the latter stopped well short of the demand for sovereignty.

Support for decentralization as a response to western alienation has been constrained in other ways. It is not clear, for instance, that a radically decentralized federal state would square with the national visions articulated in Chapter Three. If our reading of the regional political culture is correct, Western Canadians are not opposed to a reasonably strong national government; they are opposed only if that government fails to provide institutional expression for western interests and aspirations. Furthermore, there is considerable variance across the region in governmental support for decentralization, which tends to have greater appeal for the relatively wealthy provinces of Alberta and British Columbia than it does for Manitoba and Saskatchewan. The government of Saskatchewan has been particularly forceful in its defence of a strong national government.[29] For all of these reasons, then, there was not a strong regional push for decentralization throughout the constitutional debates of the 1980s and early 1990s. Provincial governments in the West joined with the government of Quebec in trying to shore up the traditional division of powers, and sought restrictions on the federal government's spending power and its ability to intrude on national resource jurisdiction. However, decentralization *per se* was not promoted with any great enthusiasm. It remained an option for the West, but not a preferred option.

But this picture may be beginning to change. One of the impacts of internationalization and globalization, and of their accompanying manifestations such as the FTA and NAFTA, is that the economic powers of the national government are becoming less relevant for Canadians. In a free trade context, governments at all levels surrender a good deal of their ability to shape the economic environment. In this context, it is not a matter of moving to the provinces economic powers which are inherently national; it is a matter of taking those powers out of the hands of all governments. Therefore, just as free trade might strengthen the logic of a sovereign Quebec, it might also strengthen the appeal of decentralization in the West. Moreover, in a period of severe fiscal constraint, the social programs of the national government are also becoming less relevant for all Canadians, including those in the West. The 1995 federal budget signalled a dramatic retreat by Ottawa from shared-cost programs and the enforcement of national standards, a retreat that sets the stage for potentially radical decentralization. It may be, then, that the western

Decentralist Alliance

To the extent that British Columbia and Alberta have pursued greater decentralization, Quebec has been an important strategic ally. They have been able to use Quebec's own agenda for a broader assault on federal powers. Columnist Rafe Mair, who served as minister of constitutional affairs in Bill Bennett's Social Credit government, makes this point for British Columbia:

> For different reasons no doubt, Quebec and British Columbia are devolutionist by nature. Each province sees decentralization of power as an important step in a continued federation. If anyone east of the Rockies needs a reason why B.C. feels so strongly this way, he need only look at the mess made of the Pacific salmon fishery by the Department of Fisheries and Oceans going back to Confederation. Indeed, most Lotuslanders feel far, far removed from the centre of power.

But what happens, then, if Quebec leaves? Mair's concern is that B.C. would be outgunned in a new and more centralized federal state: "If, God forbid, Quebec leaves the federation it will leave B.C., and I suppose Alberta as well, without a very important constitutional ally in the decentralization movement."

Rafe Mair, "B.C. Doesn't Want To Lose Its Constitutional Ally," *Financial Post*, March 3, 1995.

interest in preserving a strong national government will weaken as that government is gutted by free trade and fiscal constraint. Certainly the general regional reaction to the decentralizing thrust of the 1995 federal budget was one of support, not alarm.

Future regional support for decentralization may well depend on the outcome of constitutional developments in Quebec. If those developments push the country toward greater decentralization, or if the federal government promotes decentralization to ward off the nationalist movement in Quebec, it is unlikely that Western Canadians will buck the tide. Support may also hinge on the fate of the Reform party, which has emerged as a forceful proponent of decentralization. Preston Manning describes decentralization in the following terms:

> In practice, decentralization means putting an end to wasteful duplication between federal and provincial governments, and to intergovernmental irritants created by overlapping jurisdictions. I think I speak for everyone in Canada when I say we are all sick and tired of federal-provincial relations that resemble eleven dogs fighting over a single bone.[30]

Whether the Reform leader has caught the regional mood in this case remains to be seen.

*Senate reform*

In many respects, Senate reform would appear to offer the most appropriate institutional response to western alienation. Senates, after all, are designed, or at least should be designed, to provide an effective voice for regional interests within the national legislative process, and it is this more than anything else that Western Canadians have sought. While a reformed Senate would weaken cabinet's control of the legislative process, it would not necessarily weaken the national government within the Canadian federal state,[31] and this again is in tune with the western national visions articulated in Chapter Three. Moreover, a reformed Senate would offset the demographic weight of Ontario and Quebec, and therefore their electoral strength in the House of Commons, with a legislative institution designed to strengthen the relatively sparsely populated eastern and western peripheries. Yet despite this intrinsic appeal, the movement for Senate reform was slow to get underway in the West.

The leadership of the Senate reform movement initially came from Alberta, and from such individuals as premier Don Getty; the president of the Canada West Foundation, Dr. David Elton; and the sparkplugs for the Canadian Committee for a Triple-E Senate, Alice and Bert Brown. In 1982 the Alberta government released a reform proposal calling for a provincially appointed Senate.[32] This proposal was very much in keeping with the emphasis at the time on executive federalism, and with the push by western premiers for a more prominent provincial role in national governance. However, when a special select committee of the Alberta legislature took this proposal before public hearings across the province, they found virtually no support; replacing federal patronage with provincial patronage was of limited popular appeal. Instead, the committee found a great deal of support for the direct, popular election of senators. In light of this reaction, and in the face of mounting pressure from the Canada West Foundation and the Committee for a Triple-E Senate, the committee jettisoned the provincially appointed model and recommended that the Alberta government promote a Triple-E Senate—Elected, Equal, and Effective.[33] Despite the clear reluctance of premier Peter Lougheed to do so, the Alberta legislature and government climbed aboard the Triple-E bandwagon. When Don Getty replaced Lougheed as premier, he became the country's most enthusiastic cheerleader for the Triple-E Senate.

The Triple-E option was pushed during the dying days of the debate over the Meech Lake Accord, when the Manitoba government and opposition Liberals emerged as forceful and determined proponents. (Saskatchewan's support for Senate reform remained relatively restrained at this point, as did British Columbia's.) It was pushed again in the constitutional discussions that resulted in the 1992 Charlottetown Accord, by which time Senate reform had clearly emerged as *the* preferred solution to long-standing regional discontent. However, it too was a solution doomed to fail. From the outset there were even some reservations within the West; British Columbia had some understandable concerns about equal provincial representation in a reformed Senate, and premiers other than Alberta's Don Getty and Manitoba's Gary Filmon were often hesitant in their support. More importantly, the Triple-E model failed to find a receptive audience in Ontario and Quebec, and therefore failed to find significant support from either the Liberal or Progressive Conservative parties. The version of the Triple-E Senate that found its way into the Charlottetown Accord lacked support in Quebec where voters had no interest in provincial equality, no interest in another tier of elected federal politicians, and no interest in strengthening the effectiveness and vitality of parliamentary institutions. The inclusion of Triple-E also failed to rally support for the Accord in Western Canada, although whether this was because the reform proposal fell short of regional expectations or because Western Canadians were not prepared to accept other parts of the Accord is difficult to determine.

Throughout this period there was reasonably strong public support for Senate reform. Figure 4.2 presents a series of Gallup surveys which recorded broad national support for Senate reform, and almost no support for the status quo. It is interesting to note, however, that the most recent Gallup surveys show growing support for abolition and declining support for an elected Senate. It is also both interesting and important to note that the pattern of Western Canadian opinion on the Senate reform issue is virtually identical to that found in Ontario and Atlantic Canada. For example, the most recent Gallup survey reported in Figure 4.2 found that support for an elected Senate stood at 41 per cent in British Columbia and Atlantic Canada, and 43 per cent on the Prairies and in Ontario.[34] Support for abolition stood at 47 per cent in Atlantic Canada, and 49 per cent in Ontario and across the West. (Among Quebec respondents, 68% supported abolition and 20% supported an elected Senate.) In the 1991 Angus Reid survey, respondents were asked if they supported or opposed the "Triple-E" Senate proposal, which was defined as a Senate that would have equal *regional* representation and real constitutional powers, and would be elected by the people. In this case, support for Senate reform was strong and emphatic: 77.4 per cent said they supported the Triple-E model and only 11.8 per cent opposed it. There were no significant differences across the four western provinces in the level of support.

Although it is often assumed that Western Canadians are more supportive of Senate reform than are other Canadians, the empirical evidence shows only modest regional differences once Quebec is set aside. However, Western Canadians may still bring a different set of concerns to the Senate reform debate. Western perspectives on Senate reform have focused on the Senate's potential for more effective *regional* representation, and have been less enthusiastic about using Senate reform to address other representational issues. This difference can be illustrated through the 1992 constitutional referendum survey, in which respondents were asked if they agreed or disagreed that women should be guaranteed representation in a reformed Senate. Such a guarantee was supported by 75.8 per cent of the Quebec respondents, 63.0 per

FIGURE 4.2    Support for Senate Reform or Abolition

"Which of these things would you like to see done about the Canadian Senate—continue the present system under which the government appoints senators, elect senators as we elect Members of Parliament or do away with the Senate altogether?"

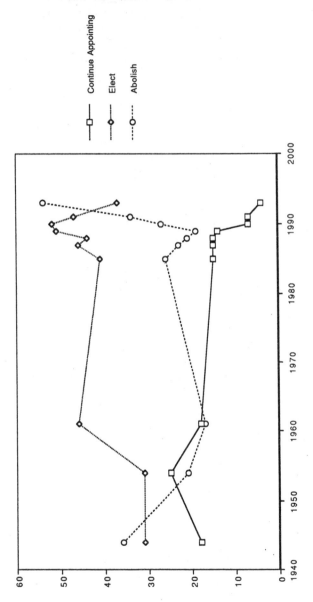

Public Support for Senate Reform

In the 1992 constitutional referendum survey, respondents were asked to choose among three options for the Senate: maintaining the status quo, reforming the Senate as proposed in the Charlottetown Accord, or abolishing it altogether. Although support for the reform option was stronger in the West than elsewhere, a plurality of Western Canadian respondents still favoured abolition.

| | Keep Senate as it is now | Reform as proposed | Abolish | Don't know |
|---|---|---|---|---|
| Atlantic | 25.6 | 24.5 | 31.1 | 18.8 |
| Quebec | 14.1 | 13.5 | 46.4 | 26.0 |
| Ontario | 19.3 | 19.5 | 41.0 | 20.2 |
| West | 15.9 | 26.5 | 36.6 | 21.0 |
| Canada | 17.4 | 20.4 | 40.3 | 21.9 |

Variation within the West was almost as great as the variation among regions. Support for the reform option captured by the Charlottetown Accord ranged from 15.8% in Saskatchewan to 25.0% in Manitoba, 25.8% in British Columbia, and 32.2% in Alberta.

cent of Atlantic respondents, and 56.1 per cent of Ontario respondents, but by only 41.6 per cent of those from Western Canada.

The defeat of the Charlottetown Accord marked the end of the Senate reform initiative. The strength of the nationalist movement in Quebec, the decentralizing drift of the federal government, and the growing assertiveness of the Ontario government in defence of provincial interests ("Ontario First!") all mean there is little chance that significant Senate reform will occur. Certainly the West will not succeed in promoting Senate reform unless reform proposals can be woven into a renewed and broader constitutional debate. Quite apart from a relatively soft governmental and public consensus on the virtues of Senate reform, the West lacks the political muscle to force Senate reform on the country. This in turn means that the fate of Senate reform, like so much else in Canada, rests on the outcome of constitutional deliberations in Quebec. If the debate on Senate reform is to be reopened, it will only be because Western Canadian proponents are able to link Senate reform to the resolution of constitutional unrest in Quebec. Given Quebec's principled and strategic opposition to Senate reform, this will not be an easy task.

*Western union*

A hypothetical response to the perceived weakness of the West in national political life would be for the four western provinces to unite into a single jurisdiction, one whose population would be larger than Quebec's. This solution, or at least variants of it, have been proposed in the past: British Columbia premier W.A.C. Bennett was an advocate of a five-regions Canada, with British Columbia as one of the regions; and the possibility of prairie union was explored at length in a 1970 conference in Lethbridge.[35] More recently, Angus Reid's 1991 Western Canada survey detected considerable support for greater cooperation among provincial governments in the West. Respondents were asked the following question:

> It has been suggested that the four western provinces—British Columbia, Alberta, Saskatchewan and Manitoba—should get together and establish common institutions or agencies to deal with certain issue areas. These common western agencies would be co-operative efforts combining resources from the four western provinces—and they would replace individual government departments currently covering those areas. What is your initial reaction to this idea—do you think it is a very good idea, moderately good, moderately bad, or very bad idea?

There was a reasonable measure of support for this suggestion, one that goes well beyond the very modest attempts at integration that have taken place to date. Across the region, 20.5 per cent thought it was a very good idea, 37.0 per cent thought it was moderately good, 23.8 per cent moderately bad, and 13.7 per cent thought it was a very bad idea. Interestingly, there were no significant differences among the provinces. However, when respondents were asked what they thought of more formal political integration, support all but vanished. Only 26.4 per cent strongly or moderately supported "combining the four western provinces to form a single Western Canadian region with one government," whereas 69.6 per cent opposed the idea. Again, there were no significant differences among the provincial respondents.

The lack of public support for formal political union is only one of many obstacles confronting this solution to western discontent. To use a regional phrase, this dog won't hunt. Neither western union nor prairie union is on the political agenda at the present time, and it is extremely unlikely that this will change in the foreseeable future. It would take nothing short of the complete restructuring of Canada in the event of Quebec's separation before any form of union would be seriously considered, and even then the existing provincial communities would be likely to survive.

CHALLENGES TO THE POLITICAL COMMUNITY

Over the past couple of decades, it has not been unheard of for people to argue that the West should "get out of Canada," that the region should "go it alone."

To this point, however, such sentiments are usually expressed in the heat of the moment; they pop up in casual conversations among friends, at the bar, or over dinner. Public opinion polls have never registered any significant level of support for an independent West, no matter how defined, and the idea has not been embraced by mainstream parties or political leaders. Even Reform has been emphatic in its support for a united Canada. Western separatism has remained at the margins of the regional political culture, and its advocates have been kept far from centre stage. In short, there has been no significant regional challenge to the national political *community*. The challenge that has come has been directed primarily to political authorities and the nature of the political regime.

Of course, there have been occasional outcroppings of support for western independence. The possibility was raised in Saskatchewan at the height of the Depression, and a 1938 poll taken by the *Regina Leader Post* showed 42 per cent in favour of secession, 47 per cent opposed, and 11 per cent undecided.[36] A flurry of small separatist movements formed in the early 1980s in the wake of the National Energy Program; two Unionist MLAs were elected in Saskatchewan and one Western Canada Concept MLA was elected in Alberta. However, when more conventional politicians bordered on separatist rhetoric, they were likely to do so out of a sense of frustration rather than a sense of commitment to the independence option. Note, for example, David Mitchell's discussion of whether W.A.C. Bennett could be considered a "proto-separatist":

> Was Bennett a kind of proto-separatist? Or was he just giving expression to the peculiar form of isolationism which was part of the Pacific coast heritage? It seems clear that he was simply exploiting a traditional Western Canadian streak of independence and resentment towards central Canada, enhanced now by B.C.'s new economic vitality. Certainly, Bennett challenged many established assumptions about Confederation, but he was always talking about improving the country, making Canada a better place to live, and he often painted himself as a kind of supernationalist.[37]

This, we would suggest, is the dominant form of "western separatism." It is frustrated Canadian nationalism, and not an endorsement of any positive vision of an independent West.

However, there is one other situation in which the rhetoric of independence is engaged, and that is to see the *threat* of independence as a strategic option. The best example comes from the 1991 Angus Reid survey in which respondents were asked if they agreed or disagreed with the following statement: "Sometimes I think the only way the West will be listened to is if we threaten to separate from the rest of Canada." As Figure 4.3 shows, 31 per cent of the respondents agreed with this statement, a proportion that was virtually the same across the region.[38] This agreement reflects a deeply embedded sense of frustration with the national government and a belief that Quebec has used the

FIGURE 4.3   Support for Western Separatism as a Strategic Option

"Do you agree or disagree with the following statement: Sometimes I think the only way the West will be listened to is if we threaten to separate from the rest of Canada."

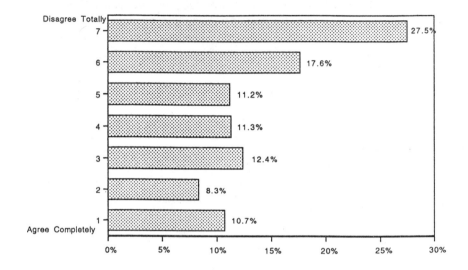

*Source*: Options for Western Canada Study, 1991

threat of separatism to extract concessions from the rest of Canada. But agreement does not reflect the belief that the West *should* separate, or that the West would be better off on its own. As in the case of W.A.C. Bennett, expressions of separatism are best seen as a frustrated sense of Canadian nationalism, something that is dramatically different from the situation in Quebec.

But will this continue to be the case in the years to come, or will the existence of the national community come up for more general and intense debate? This could conceivably happen if Western Canadians remain frustrated in their search for institutional reform, as they are likely to be, or if the search for more effective partisan leverage on the federal government also fails, as it is likely to do. Although even intense frustration in the past did not result in serious challenge to the political community, this cannot be guaranteed in the future. However, the much more likely probability is that events in Quebec will open up a Western Canadian debate about the future of the West in Canada, be that Canada inclusive or exclusive of Quebec. If this assumption is correct, then we must first turn to the relationship between the West and Quebec before we can address the future of the West in Canada. The former is tackled in the next chapter; the latter in Chapter Six.

NOTES

1. As argued elsewhere, western alienation is quite different in character from most other forms of political alienation. Unlike the general case, it has not been associated with the usual clientele of alienation—the dispossessed, the poor, or those at the economic and social margins. See Gibbins, *Prairie Politics & Society: Regionalism in Decline* (Toronto: Butterworths, 1980), pp. 167-8.
2. David Easton, *A Framework for Political Analysis* (Englewood Cliffs, N.J.: Prentice-Hall, 1965).
3. Steve Dorey, *Free Trade on the Prairies* (Regina: Canadian Plains Research Center, 1989), p. 1.
4. *Ibid.*
5. It is interesting to note that nationalists in Quebec supported the free trade agreements for somewhat similar political reasons. The agreements would make federal economic policy, and therefore Ottawa, less relevant for the lives and future of Quebecers.
6. Dorey, *Free Trade*, p. 108.
7. The proportion of respondents expecting their provincial economy to be hurt over the longer term ranged from 56.3% in Manitoba to 53.6% in British Columbia, 49.9% in Saskatchewan, and 37.2% in Alberta.
8. Cited in Jeffrey Simpson, *Faultlines: Struggling for a Canadian Vision* (Toronto: HarperCollins, 1993), p. 133.
9. Whether western loyalty would have paid off in 1979 when the Joe Clark Conservatives formed a minority government is impossible to assess, given the quick defeat of the Clark government.
10. Simpson, *Faultlines*, p. 113.
11. David E. Smith, *Building a Province: A History of Saskatchewan in Documents* (Saskatoon: Fifth House Publishers, 1992), p. 368.
12. For example, see J.F. Conway, *The West: The History of a Region in Confederation* (Toronto: James Lorimer, 1994), pp. 327-9.
13. For example, see Tom Flanagan, *Waiting for the Wave: The Reform Party and Preston Manning* (Toronto: Stoddart, 1995); S.M. Lipset, *Agrarian Socialism: The Cooperative Commonwealth Federation in Saskatchewan*, rev. ed. (New York: Doubleday, 1968); J.R.

Mallory, *Social Credit and the Federal Power in Canada* (Toronto: University of Toronto Press, 1954); W.L. Morton, *The Progressive Party of Canada* (Toronto: University of Toronto Press, 1950); and Walter D. Young, *The Anatomy of a Party: The National CCF 1932-61* (Toronto: University of Toronto Press, 1970).

14. It is important that readers not confuse the Progressives and the Conservatives. The latter did not become the *Progressive* Conservatives until 1942, by which time the former had disappeared as a national party.

15. Richard Allen, *The Social Passion* (Toronto: University of Toronto Press, 1973).

16. For a discussion of Reform's decision to "go national," see Flanagan, *Waiting for the Wave*, ch. 5.

17. David Lewis and Frank R. Scott, *Make This Your Canada* (Toronto, 1943), p. 104.

18. Here it is important to note the distorting effect of the electoral system. Although Ontario accounted for only 7% of the seats won by the CCF between 1935 and 1958, it accounted for 34% of the party's total popular vote.

19. C.B. Macpherson, *Democracy in Alberta: Social Credit and the Party System* (Toronto: University of Toronto Press, 1953), pp. 215-6.

20. David Laycock, "Reforming Canadian Democracy? Institutions and Ideology in the Reform Party Project," *Canadian Journal of Political Science*, xxvii: 2 (June 1994), pp. 233-9.

21. For a discussion of the British case, see Keith Archer *et al.*, *Parameters of Power: Canada's Political Institutions* (Toronto: Nelson, 1995), pp. 201-2.

22. Thomas Peterson, "Manitoba: Ethnic and Class Politics," in Martin Robin, ed., *Canadian Provincial Politics*, 2nd ed. (Scarborough: Prentice-Hall, 1978).

23. David E. Smith, *Prairie Liberalism: The Liberal Party in Saskatchewan, 1905-1971* (Toronto: University of Toronto Press, 1975), p. 324.

24. Manitoba passed an "Initiative and Referendum" law in 1916.

25. This statement was less correct historically when Ottawa could infringe through its power to reserve or disallow provincial legislation even if such legislation fell within the exclusive jurisdiction of the province. This power is now a constitutional dead letter. The statement is also incorrect to the extent that the federal government is prepared to use its spending power to shape provincial programs and priorities, something the current government signalled in the 1995 budget that it is no longer prepared to do.

26. Joe Clark, *A Nation Too Good To Lose* (Toronto: Key Porter Books, 1994), pp. 216-8.

27. David J. Mitchell, *WAC: Bennett and the Rise of British Columbia* (Vancouver: Douglas & McIntyre, 1983), p. 349.

28. *The Gallup Report*, May 18, 1992.

29. For examples of such a defence, see Smith, *Building a Province*, pp. 419, 423, 424 and 443.

30. Preston Manning, "A New and Better Home for Canadians," keynote address to the Reform Party Assembly, Ottawa, October 15, 1994.

31. In Australia and the United States, strong Senates co-exist with relatively centralized federal states. In both cases, the argument can be made that the strength of the Senate facilitated the growth of the national government, that Senates have been centralizing in effect if not necessarily in design. For a discussion of the American case, see Gibbins, *Regionalism: Territorial Politics in Canada and the United States* (Toronto: Butterworths, 1982), ch. 3.

32. Government of Alberta, *A Provincially Appointed Senate: A New Federalism for Canada* (Edmonton: 1982).

33. Special Select Committee of the Alberta Legislature, *Strengthening Canada* (Edmonton: Government of Alberta, 1985).

34. *The Gallup Report*, July 22, 1993.

35. David K. Elton, ed., *One Prairie Province?* (Lethbridge: Lethbridge Herald, 1970).

36. Cited in Conway, *The West*, p. 151.

37. Mitchell, *WAC*, p. 351.

38. The highest level of agreement was in Alberta (33.3%), but the level of agreement in the remaining three provinces was very similar: 32.1% in British Columbia, 29.0% in Saskatchewan, and 28.1% in Manitoba.

# CHAPTER FIVE

# Quebec and the West

At first glance, one might not expect a great deal of interaction between Quebec and the West. After all, the two regions are separated by Ontario and, to a significant degree, exist within quite distinct linguistic and cultural environments. Within Quebec, Western Canadian events, issues, and concerns have a very low profile in both the mass media and popular culture. And yet, while the West may not be all that relevant to Quebecers as they try to sort out their future inside or outside Canada, Quebec is very relevant to the West. Indeed, the West as a contemporary political region exists in large part as a counterpoint to Quebec and to the challenge that Quebec has posed to the Canadian community and its institutions. The political climate created by Quebec's challenge makes it easier for all Canadians, including Western Canadians, to see the West as a coherent region rather than as a loose collection of four distinct provinces. In this sense, "the West" is a byproduct of Quebec's ongoing challenge to the Canadian state.

The assertion that Quebec provides the "glue" for Western Canada will strike many readers as provocative, if not offensive, and we want to be quick to point out that Quebec is not the only glue holding the region together. More general tensions between the West and Central Canada, and between the West and the federal government, have also been important, although Quebec-related tensions are a component of both. However, it has been the prolonged crisis over the place of Quebec within the federation that has created the stage upon which Western Canadian leaders have articulated the national visions discussed in Chapter Three. Quebec's unrest has not only provided this stage, but has also forced western politicians to address constitutional principles and reforms, and to constitutionalize grievances and visions which otherwise might have been tackled by more conventional political action. The stimulus of Quebec's discontent, therefore, has provided both a challenge and an opportunity.

A useful analogy, and one employed frequently by Reform leader Preston Manning, is that of surfing. Western leaders have been surfers on the waves of discontent generated by the nationalist movement in Quebec. Western discontent alone is incapable of generating waves of sufficient magnitude to wash ashore with any effect in Ottawa or Central Canada, where regional discontent on the peripheries is seen at worst as a minor irritant. At times, however, western leaders have been able to ride the Quebec waves to their own advantage. There is little question, for example, that while the 1982 Constitution Act was a response to discontent in Quebec, it had a better fit with core constitutional values in the West than it did with those in Quebec.[1] It is in this context that Manning once described Quebec's discontent as an opportunity for his party and for the West more generally: "Reformers welcome the current constitutional ferment in Quebec because it will crack the Canadian Constitution wide open and force the rest of Canada to address the task of developing a new one, rather than attempting to patch up the old one."[2] Although Reformers have since found that the Constitution presents treacherous terrain for their party, and for that matter all parties, the basic conclusion remains: it is Quebec's discontent that gives the West some leverage on the evolution of Canadian federalism.

Of course, the relationship between the two regions is not always symbiotic, and Quebec's constitutional aspirations have often run counter to constitutional visions articulated in the West. As the discussion in Chapter Three demonstrated, such differences have been brought into bold relief in recent years. There is, therefore, a need for western politicians to be active participants in the broader constitutional debate, for without their participation Canada could well be shaped along lines that would leave Western Canadians uncomfortable and potentially disadvantaged within their own country. Although participation guarantees neither success nor popularity at home, as western premiers found to their chagrin during the Meech Lake episode, it is impossible to avoid. Thus Quebec's unrest has provided more than an opportunity; it has provided an essential prod for Western Canadians, for all Canadians, to think through the future of their country. But, as they do so, it is also impossible to avoid coming to grips with Quebec's discontent, and with the future of Quebec in Canada. For better or for worse, the fate of the West is inextricably tied to constitutional developments in Quebec.

QUEBEC AND THE SETTLEMENT OF THE WEST

The West's entanglement with Quebec has deep historical roots even though, when Confederation was put into place in 1867, the region did not exist as a recognized political community. The regional landmass still rested in the hands of the British Crown and the Hudson's Bay Company;[3] Manitoba did not enter Confederation until 1870, followed by British Columbia in 1871 and the creation of Alberta and Saskatchewan in 1905. At the time of the first post-Confederation census in 1871, only three per cent of the national population lived west of the Manitoba-Ontario border, compared to 32 per cent who lived in Quebec. Thus while the place of Quebec within the Canadian federal state was a central concern in the debate over Confederation, there was no one at the table to speak for the West. The three Prairie provinces were products of rather than participants in the original Confederation agreement, British Columbians were not engaged in the negotiations, and Aboriginal peoples were not recognized as legitimate members of the political community. To the extent that the West was present in discussions leading up to the formation of Canada, it was there primarily as an economic dream for Central Canadians. Note, for example, an editorial that appeared in the Toronto *Globe* on March 6, 1862:

> When [the West] belongs to Canada, when its navigable waters are traversed for a few years by vessels, and lines of travel are permanently established, when settlements are formed in favourable locations throughout the territory, it will not be difficult by grants of land to secure the construction of a railway across the plains and through the mountains.... If we set about the work of opening the territory at once, we shall win the race [against the United States] .... It is an empire we have in view, and its whole export and import trade will be concentrated in the hands of Canadian merchants and manufacturers if we strike for it now.[4]

The West, however, was important in another sense of more immediate relevance to the present discussion. For French Canadians, the settlement of the West, and particularly the prairie West, was the litmus test for the evolving nature of the Canadian state. Simply put, they watched to see if settlement would follow the bicultural pattern that had been implicit in the Confederation agreement,[5] or if it would mark out new demographic and cultural directions for Canada. If the West was to present the "new face" of Canada, what would that face be? Would French Canadians feel at home within the new provinces, would their language and culture be secure, or would the settlement of the West reinforce the growing isolation of francophones within Quebec?

In part the test turned out to be less than fair, since few French Canadians relocated in Western Canada. Indeed, for every one person who moved from Quebec to the West before 1931, including many who were Quebec anglophones, six moved to the West from Ontario and eight moved from Quebec to the United States.[6] (Quebec's political leadership, fearing the province's depopulation, discouraged emigration to the West or elsewhere.) The relatively small number of French Canadians who did move to the West presented a difficult conundrum for provincial governments trying to assimilate a large and polyglot immigrant population. Those governments, and for that matter their constituents, were prone to treat the regional francophone population as just another minority, and a somewhat small minority at that; constitutional provisions which indicated otherwise were overlooked or ignored.[7] In political terms, French Canadians were viewed from the perspective of their regional electoral strength; Quebec's much more potent federal electoral strength was ignored. Special rights or protections for French Canadians were seen as

**Table 5.1**

Mother Tongue of Western Canadian Population

|      | English | French | Other |
|------|---------|--------|-------|
| 1921 | 68.3    | 4.7    | 27.0  |
| 1931 | 62.4    | 4.0    | 33.6  |
| 1941 | 63.3    | 4.3    | 32.4  |
| 1951 | 69.9    | 3.9    | 26.2  |
| 1961 | 72.9    | 3.4    | 23.7  |
| 1971 | 76.5    | 2.9    | 20.6  |
| 1976 | 79.4    | 2.6    | 18.0  |
| 1981 | 79.8    | 2.7    | 17.5  |
| 1986 | 79.5    | 2.1    | 18.4  |
| 1991 | 79.6    | 2.1    | 18.3  |

Source: Canada Census

problematic because they could impede the assimilation of the non-British, non-French immigrant communities. These communities, which were individually and collectively larger than the French-Canadian communities on the Prairies, could potentially claim any educational or linguistic protections provided for French Canadians. And the assimilated immigrants themselves, who had paid a high personal price by learning a new language and acclimatizing themselves to a very different cultural environment, had little sympathy for French Canadians whom they saw as unwilling to pay a similar price.

Table 5.1 shows that the proportion of the Western Canadian population reporting a French mother tongue (language first learned as a child and still understood as an adult) has been small throughout this century, and has been steadily shrinking. There have been significant pockets of francophones in the West, and some variance in strength across the four provinces, but nowhere has the proportion of francophones come close to matching the proportion of the regional population whose mother tongue is neither English nor French. At the time of the 1991 census, Manitoba had the highest proportion of residents with a French mother tongue (4.3%), and British Columbia had the lowest (1.9%). However, no matter how the census data is viewed, one conclusion is inescapable: individuals whose mother tongue is French constitute an insignificant and declining *demographic* component of Western Canadian society.

Perhaps the most fundamental problem was that French Canadians on the Prairies ran up against regional values which assigned them at best a peripheral role. As outlined in Chapter Three, the dominant western visions of recent decades have been based on the equality of individuals and on a form of multiculturalism that gives no pride of place to French Canadians.[8] The multicultural western population rejected visions of Canada which emphasized its binational character or gave special recognition to two founding peoples. Note, for example, Saskatchewan premier Allan Blakeney's 1977 comment to the Task Force on Canadian Unity:

> ... many brave words have been spoken about the advantages of living in a country with two cultural traditions. Once again, that is a point of view which makes sense in Central Canada, but has much less meaning for Saskatchewan. The distance between Regina and Montreal is greater than the distance between Paris and Moscow. Very few residents of Saskatchewan have experienced francophone culture at first hand. The French fact in Saskatchewan continues to be a matter of bilingual labels and a small community of francophones, smaller by far than the communities of German or Ukrainian speakers.[9]

This theme has been picked up by Denis Smith, who observed that "the prairie difficulty in accustoming itself to bilingualism and biculturalism is not simply bigotry: it is deeply entrenched policy that emerges from the prairie attempt to establish its own identity."[10] Of necessity, that identity was based on the assimilation of ethnic minorities into a composite rather than bicultural Canadian nationality. It was precisely because of the ethnic mosaic of prairie settlement that the Canadian nationalism that emerged was similar in spirit to the melting-pot nationalism commonly associated with the United States.

In this context, the "One Canada" nationalism of John Diefenbaker was a faithful reflection of his prairie roots:

> We shall never build the nation which our potential resources make possible by dividing ourselves into Anglophones, Francophones, multicultural-phones, or whatever kind of phoneys you choose. I say: Canadians, first, last, and always![11]

Diefenbaker was the first Canadian prime minister with an ethnic background that was in part neither British nor French, and as such he was "determined to bring about a Canadian citizenship that knew no hyphenated consideration."[12] Nonetheless, it is difficult to imagine a nationalist creed that would provoke more hostility from Quebec nationalists than did Diefenbaker's "One Canada," even though it was a creed that enjoyed reasonable support among French Canadians in Diefenbaker's Saskatchewan heartland.[13]

All this should not suggest, of course, that Quebec and the West have always been at loggerheads. While conflict has often been intense, it has also been episodic. Nor were the issues under dispute restricted to the West, although conflict may have been amplified in the region. The debate over French language education rights in Ontario, for example, has been no less

John Diefenbaker and Quebec

Western Canadian hostility towards Quebec is often associated with former prime minister John Diefenbaker. However, while Diefenbaker's "One Canada" vision is admittedly difficult to reconcile with the visions advanced by Quebec nationalists, it is unfair to assume that Diefenbaker opposed Quebec's interests across the board. It was his government that introduced simultaneous translation to the House of Commons, and Diefenbaker was the first non-French-Canadian prime minister to address the Quebec electorate in French, thereby demonstrating his personal respect for the French language and culture. As one of his biographers admits, the results were at best mixed:

> ... the reaction of French-Canadian audiences was compounded of horror at the Chief's brand of French and awe that he was even attempting it. The Chief seemed to share some of the horror as he struggled along; and eventually Quebec audiences accepted his French as a strange but impressive convulsion of nature, part of the national landscape, like Montmorency Falls.[14]

In Diefenbaker's case, and more generally, opposition to Quebec's political agenda and the province's national power cannot be equated with hostility to French Canadians, although Quebecers could be excused if they were to miss this distinction!

contentious than the similar debate in Western Canada. Some of the regional conflict, moreover, has been over national policy and has had similar dynamics across the country. The conflict between French and English Canadians over the use of military conscription in the First and Second World Wars was intense in the West, but probably no more so than elsewhere in the country. Admittedly, western reaction, when seen in isolation, may look extreme. Note, for example, a comment by journalist Bob Edwards in the *Calgary Eye Opener*. Edwards was discussing Liberal leader Sir Wilfrid Laurier's opposition to the use of conscription in the First World War, and asked his readers if they were

> going to let this hoary four-flusher get away with this? Not on your tintype! Canada shall not desert her defenders to please any whited Sepulchre from Quebec.... One would almost imagine that Wilfrid as a child had been raised on sauerkraut instead of pea soup.[15]

Yet similar statements could readily be found within the Atlantic and Ontario press of the same era.[16] The Western Canadian response to the conscription crises, therefore, was characteristic of a broader English-Canadian response.

Nonetheless, from Quebec's standpoint, and from the more general standpoint of French Canadians, the western "experiment" was a failure. The regional population that emerged was multicultural rather than bicultural, was soon to become overwhelmingly anglophone in composition, and was opposed in principle and practice to the protection of linguistic or cultural minorities, including French Canadians. The settlement of the West, therefore, increased the already growing linguistic and cultural isolation of Quebec. It also ensured that there would be ongoing tension between the West and a federal government within which Quebec politicians and interests consistently outmuscled those from the West.

BILINGUALISM AND BICULTURALISM

In 1965 Prime Minister Lester Pearson established the Royal Commission on Bilingualism and Biculturalism. Perhaps inadvertently, the Commission touched off a thirty-year struggle to recast the constitutional and institutional definition of the Canadian state in light of the growing nationalist movement in Quebec (the "wave" referred to previously). The Commission's mandate was to find a federalist alternative to this movement, one that was energized by the Quiet Revolution and was beginning to flirt with separatism. However, the Commission was also to set the stage for protracted conflict between national visions emerging from Quebec and the West. In this conflict Western Canadians won some important battles but, they suspect, may have lost the war.[17] The irony is that Quebec nationalists came to precisely the same conclusion: that Quebec won some of the battles but lost the war. The Canadian "vision" that was to emerge later in constitutional proposals such as the Meech Lake and Charlottetown Accords was a delicate balance that found only minority support in either Quebec or the West.

The recommendations of the Royal Commission were to leave an indelible imprint on the country. In the initial deliberations and conceptual design of the Commission, bilingualism and biculturalism were envisioned as two faces of the same coin. Language was seen as the essential vehicle for cultural expression, and therefore bilingualism was important not only in its own right but also as a means by which the bicultural character of Canada could be expressed and sustained. As it turned out, however, the federal government, led at the time of the Commission's report by Prime Minister Pierre Trudeau, rejected this linkage between language and culture. Instead, the government opted for *multiculturalism* within a *bilingual framework*. The linkage the Commission took for granted between language and culture was broken, and bilingualism was pursued without any corresponding adoption of a bicultural conception of Canada. The country's commitment to bilingualism was expressed in the 1969 Official Languages Act, and was then constitutionally entrenched in the language provisions of the 1982 Constitution Act. The commitment to multiculturalism was expressed legislatively in the 1971

Multiculturalism Act, and received constitutional recognition in section 27 of the 1982 Charter of Rights and Freedoms, which states that "This Charter shall be interpreted in a manner consistent with the preservation and enhancement of the multicultural heritage of Canadians."

The rejection of biculturalism and the country's subsequent embrace of multiculturalism was an important victory for multicultural communities in Canada, and particularly for those in the West who mounted sustained lobbying pressure on the Royal Commission and government of the day. At the same time, it was a major setback for those Quebec nationalists who were still committed to Canada but who saw the country's foundation as a contractual agreement between two cultural communities, and who argued that the preservation of French required the collective protection of Quebec's distinct society. However, it was not necessarily a setback for French Canadians more broadly defined, for the adoption of official bilingualism spoke to the expansive, pan-Canadian form of French Canadian nationalism articulated near the turn of the century by Henri Bourassa. Writing in 1912, Bourassa asserted:

> We deserve better than ...to be told: "Remain in Quebec, continue to stagnate in ignorance, you are at home there; but elsewhere you must become English." No, we have the right to be French in language; we have the right to be Catholic in faith; we have the right to be free by the Constitution. We are Canadians before all; and we have the right to be as British as anyone. And we have the right to enjoy these rights throughout the whole expanse of Confederation.[18]

More generally, the implementation of the Royal Commission's recommendations was a clear win for official language minorities, both English and French.

The adoption of bilingualism was of critical importance to francophones residing outside Quebec, including those in the West. Nonetheless, the choice of multiculturalism rather than biculturalism implicitly reduced French Canadians to the status of one cultural minority among many, and thus weakened any symbolic or constitutional claims stemming from their founding status. It was an important turning point in the definition of Canada, one that was to make Canada less and Quebec more attractive to those determined to preserve the cultural integrity of French Canada. For their part, Western Canadians placed far less emphasis on the adoption of multiculturalism than they did on the imposition of bilingualism. While the former constituted significant symbolic recognition, it was light with respect to its impact on public policy and programs; the latter's impact was direct and significant in both respects. Therefore the delicate compromise between bilingualism and multiculturalism that the Trudeau government tried to achieve was seen as nothing of the sort by most Western Canadians, who objected strenuously to the French language being "shoved down their throats." Hence the irony: the compromise was satisfactory neither to Quebec nationalists nor to Western Canadians, each of whom focused more on their loss than on their gain.

Yet none of this should suggest that discontent with official bilingualism has been restricted to the West. A Gallup poll conducted in May 1991 found that 63 per cent of the national sample felt bilingualism had been a failure, and in this instance Western Canadian opinion (64% on the Prairies and 71% in British Columbia) was very much in line with opinion in Ontario, where 64 per cent of the respondents considered bilingualism a failure.[19] In April 1994, the national Angus Reid Poll asked a representative sample of 1,470 adult Canadians the following question: "Officially, Canada is a bilingual country with both English and French as official languages. What do you think about official bilingualism? Would you say you strongly support, moderately support, moderately oppose, or strongly oppose official bilingualism?" In this case, the West did stand apart, although the differences were not huge. Across the region, 48 per cent supported official bilingualism (either strongly or moderately), compared to 58 per cent in Ontario, 73 per cent in Atlantic Canada, and 88 per cent in Quebec. What is important to note is not only the distinctive character of western opinion, but also the relative intensity of opposition. Across the West, 32 per cent of respondents strongly opposed official bilingualism, a proportion that compares to 22 per cent of Ontario respondents and 12 per cent of those in Atlantic Canada. The intensity of regional opposition is reflected in Figure 5.1, which presents data from the 1991 Angus Reid survey.

Three years later, opinions toward bilingualism varied significantly among the western provinces, as Table 5.2 shows. Somewhat surprisingly, Albertans stood apart through their relative support for bilingualism. The 1994 Angus Reid poll also asked if official bilingualism should be scrapped because "it's expensive and inefficient," or whether it is worth keeping "as an important principle" for the country. Across English Canada, 50 per cent favoured scrapping bilingualism and 47 per cent favoured keeping it; in British Columbia and Manitoba/Saskatchewan respectively, 61 per cent and 66 per cent favoured scrapping official bilingualism.

Given that opposition to bilingualism has been such a flashpoint of regional discontent, and that it has figured so prominently in national depictions of Western Canada, it is useful to take a moment to examine this issue in more detail. Western Canadians may well recognize that official bilingualism serves a positive objective, and that is to increase the participation of francophones in national public life and to enhance the level of comfort francophones feel across the country. However, they also assert that there is a critical downside to bilingualism: that it makes career mobility within the federal public service, and within many professional and political associations, more difficult for those coming from a unilingual, anglophone environment such as the one that prevails across the West. In short, official bilingualism tips employment and career opportunities toward those individuals most likely to have been raised

FIGURE 5.1   Support for Official Bilingualism

"Officially, Canada is a bilingual country with both English and French as official languages. What do you think about official bilingualism? Would you say you strongly support, moderately support, moderately oppose, or strongly oppose official bilingualism?"

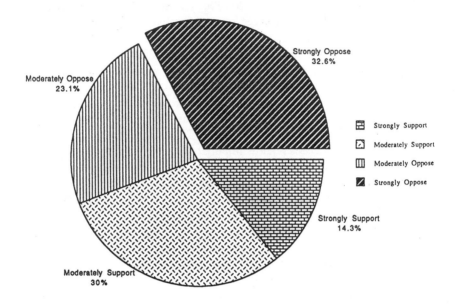

*Source*: Options for Western Canada Study, 1991

**Table 5.2**

Regional Support for Official Bilingualism

|  | *Strongly Support* | *Moderately Support* | *Moderately Oppose* | *Strongly Oppose* |
|---|---|---|---|---|
| B.C. | 14 | 30 | 22 | 33 |
| Alberta | 15 | 44 | 16 | 23 |
| Sask/Manitoba | 8 | 32 | 19 | 40 |
| Ontario | 24 | 34 | 20 | 22 |
| Quebec | 57 | 31 | 7 | 5 |
| Atlantic | 36 | 37 | 14 | 12 |
| Canada | 30% | 34% | 16% | 19% |

Source: Angus Reid Survey, 1994

in a bilingual environment, who in turn come predominantly from Quebec and, within Quebec, from Montreal. Bilingual individuals outside Quebec also share in these employment advantages to a significant and perhaps even greater degree, and may thereby assume an elite status within their own province.[20] Official bilingualism therefore has redistributive consequences that often are not acknowledged: francophones become more comfortable in Canada, and unilingual anglophones from Western Canada become less comfortable as the Canadian ideal becomes defined in ways to which most Western Canadians cannot aspire. But—and here is the essential point—it is not the policy's fairness that is the major source of grievance; it is that any dissent is branded as illegitimate and prejudiced. This conclusion is neatly summarized by Don Braid who, at the time, was a columnist with *The Edmonton Journal*:

> Bilingualism has become a ritual chant.... they [a self-satisfied ruling elite] demand it of national leaders, thus guaranteeing their continued membership in the club. They dismiss dissenters as red-necked bigots and intellectual lightweights, while exercising a powerful bigotry of their own.[21]

Western Canadians have not only confronted policies that increase their own marginalization within Canada, but are also told that any form of dissent is bigotry. The clear implication is that they should not only put up, but shut up. And, at the same time, they are told that it is perfectly legitimate for an individual dedicated to the destruction of Canada to be Leader of Her Majesty's Loyal Opposition. Some degree of head-scratching seems appropriate in these circumstances.

Robert Mason Lee,

"Please don't tell Westerners to shut up about the referendum"

"The elites are back. Westerners hoped they had disappeared with the Charlottetown accord, but they're still among us.... Once again, the elites are defining the limits of acceptable debate. And once again, their attempts will most certainly backfire...

There is little for the elites to fear from plain talk out of the West. But the smile had barely leaped to PQ Leader Parizeau's lips on Monday [following the PQ's 1994 election win] than the elites were telling the West to shut its mouth. From Prime Minister Jean Chrétien on down, they warned against saying anything that might inflame Quebec or work to the separatists' advantage. Mr. Parizeau will try to provoke you, the elites warned, don't rise to the bait.

I wonder if the elites paused to consider how deeply patronizing that sounded, to the West and Quebec alike. I wonder if they know what fools they appear to take us for. Probably not. They would chafe at a similar muzzle if it were placed on them, even if it were warranted in their case.

Without apologies to the wishes of the elite, the West intends to be a full participant in the Quebec referendum. There may be harsh words exchanged, there may be pitch and woo, but at least the debate will have the benefit of honesty. Quebec and the West have less to fear from each other than from the syrupy-voiced elites, who would deny them their history, their voice, their experience."

*Globe and Mail*, September 17, 1994, p. D2.

Braid's viewpoint was framed more generally by John Diefenbaker in a 1963 debate in the House of Commons. Diefenbaker expressed a common frustration among Western Canadians that *any* criticism of Quebec is assumed to reflect unreasoned hostility to Quebec, or to French Canadians more generally:

The suggestion has been made that I am anti-Quebec because I dared to say that I disagreed with Premier Lesage. Is he anti-Canadian because he disagrees with me? Was he anti-Quebec when he disagreed with Premier Duplessis? Surely there must be better arguments advanced than that, that every time you disagree with the Premier of one province in Canada you thereby become anti-Quebec. I was never anti-Quebec at any time.[22]

But Diefenbaker's protestations carried little weight, and criticisms of

Quebec today are still seen to violate the taboos of political debate in Canada, if only for the strategic reason that they are thought to encourage support for Quebec sovereigntists. To criticize Quebec is to inflame nationalism in Quebec, which is to make the destruction of Canada more likely, and thus criticisms are anti-Canadian. A recent example of this line of reasoning is provided by Paul McKeague in a column written for the Montreal *Gazette*:

> Who's a bigger threat to Canadian unity: Lucien Bouchard or Preston Manning? As leader of the separatist Bloc Québécois, Bouchard is usually portrayed as the great enemy of Confederation in the Commons. But Manning may actually pose a graver danger to those committed to keeping Canada together. The Reform Party leader is in many ways better positioned than Bouchard to create national divisions and stir up hostilities between Quebec and the rest of the country.[23]

Criticisms of the West, however, are fair game as regional alienation is not seen to pose a significant threat to national survival.

THE REGIONAL GRIEVANCE EXPLORED

In coming to grips with Western Canadian opinion towards Quebec, it is essential to ask a basic question: on balance, are Western Canadians simply hostile towards or, not to put too fine a point on it, prejudiced against *French Canadians*? In other words, is regional opposition to special status for Quebec rooted in the prejudice and ill-will of individuals in the West? And, if so, are Western Canadians distinctive in this respect?

These are not questions to be answered quickly. There is no reason to believe that Western Canadians are free of prejudice, and when we look at issues such as the use of turbans within the RCMP, there may be anecdotal evidence suggesting that Western Canadians are disproportionately prone to some forms of discriminatory attitudes. Moreover, the political opinions that Western Canadians hold with respect to Quebec are undoubtedly laced with disparaging stereotypes. As Don Braid and Sydney Sharpe observe, "Westerners regard Quebec politics as inherently more venal than the western variety, despite ample evidence of lusty trough-snorting in their own region."[24] However, it is our assertion that the basic answer to these questions is "no"; regional antagonism *to Quebec* is not rooted in the prejudice *toward French Canadians*. The prejudice that exists among some individual Western Canadians, and perhaps even among many, does not go to the core of regional attitudes toward Quebec. Western hostility is directly primarily toward Quebec as a political entity, and not to French Canadians or to the individual residents of Quebec. More specifically, it is directed to the disproportionate power and influence that Quebec is seen to exercise within the Canadian federal state and its national government. As a number of empirical studies have shown,[25] antipathy toward Quebec rather than toward French Canadians pro-

Gable, *The Globe and Mail*, October 10, 1994, p. A16:

Reprinted with permission from *The Globe and Mail*.

vides the best explanation for the degree of western alienation expressed by individuals.

The dominant belief in the West during the time of public controversy over official bilingualism was that Canada had embarked upon a course that would give greater and greater emphasis to the interests of Quebec, and correspondingly less emphasis to the regional grievances of the West. This belief was reinforced by the weakness of the Liberal party in Western Canada, and by Prime Minister Trudeau's insensitivity to and impatience with regional differences within "English Canada." As Table 5.3 shows, the Liberal dominance of the national government from 1965 through the 1980 election was sustained by solid support in Quebec, and the Liberals were neither weakened nor troubled by their inability to capture more than a handful of Western Canadian seats. (The exception to the Liberals' dismal regional track record was the 1968 election, when Trudeaumania rippled across Canada and throughout the West.) The almost complete rejection of the Liberal party by the West was of no significant consequence for the Liberals' grip on national power, but it was to increasingly isolate the region in parliamentary politics. Not surprisingly, the federal government came to be seen increasingly by those west of Ontario as an instrument through which Quebec could exercise undue influence on national affairs, a perception reinforced when the Trudeau Liberals campaigned in Quebec on the basis of "French power" in Ottawa, and when Quebec governments promoted the virtues of "profitable federalism." This should not suggest, incidentally, that Western Canadians had lost sight of Ontario as an ongoing source of regional concern. In some ways, the ascendancy of Quebec's influence strengthened Ontario's leverage on national economic policy, or at least did so when the economic interests of the two Central Canadian provinces coincided. The nadir in the relationship between the West and the federal government, and particularly between Alberta and the federal government, came in 1980 when Ottawa introduced the National Energy Program. In this case, Ontario and Quebec had a common interest in maintaining a low domestic price for oil, an interest not shared by most of the western provinces.

During the 1970s, the conflict between the West and the federal government paralleled to some degree that between the Quebec and federal governments. In both cases, provincial governments sought to ward off federal intrusions, and to shore up provincial influence in the emerging institutions of executive federalism. Then, in 1980, and on the heels of the re-election of the Trudeau Liberals and the defeat of the Quebec referendum on sovereignty-association, both conflicts spilled over into the constitutional arena. The Prime Minister had promised Quebecers that, should they vote "no" in the referendum, then the federal government would reform the Constitution to provide for "renewed federalism." This promise touched off fifteen years of constitutional debate that stretched from ministerial meetings in the summer of 1980 through to the Constitution Act of 1982, the 1987 Meech Lake Accord,

**Table 5.3**

Liberal Success in Federal Elections, 1965-1980

| | Quebec | | Western Canada | |
|---|---|---|---|---|
| | # seats | % vote | # seats | % vote |
| 1965 (Liberals win nationally) | 57 | 45.6 | 8 | 27.0 |
| 1968 (Liberals win nationally) | 56 | 53.6 | 27 | 37.4 |
| 1972 (Liberals win nationally) | 56 | 49.1 | 7 | 27.5 |
| 1974 (Liberals win nationally) | 60 | 54.1 | 13 | 29.6 |
| 1979 (Liberals lose nationally) | 67 | 61.7 | 3 | 22.6 |
| 1980 (Liberals win nationally) | 74 | 68.2 | 2 | 23.4 |

the 1992 Charlottetown Accord, and the subsequent national referendum. This protracted, often acrimonious, and in many respects unsuccessful debate brought the national visions of Quebec and the West into sharper contrast, and drove a deep wedge between the two regions.

The perception that Quebec exercises disproportionate power in Canadian political life is a basic feature of the way in which Western Canadians see the world, one that complements rather than negates an equally strong belief about Ontario's power.[26] Note, for example, the 1971 frustration of British Columbia premier W.A.C. Bennett at the federal government's refusal to assist in the funding of the Yellowhead Highway stretching across north-central British Columbia and Alberta: "They are a negative little group down there. We haven't got a Canadian government—it's a Quebec government."[27] More than twenty years later, Joe Clark reflected on the same theme:

> ... there is a real and growing resentment of the idea that Canada's agenda is being driven by Quebec. That resentment is not inherently anti-Quebec, although it has stoked that sentiment. Seen more constructively, it is a demand that the urgent priorities of other Canadians be given serious attention too, and not be short-changed by a preoccupation with Quebec.[28]

Western Canadians draw attention to the predominance of Quebecers at the peaks of national life. There is a long-standing belief that the national parties cater to the Quebec electorate, and that Quebec more than any other province has the capacity to make or break a national government. (True, Quebec voters did not have this capacity in 1993, but they still provided the prime minister, the entire official Opposition, and a significant chunk of the federal cabinet.) Western Canadians point to a protracted constitutional debate fixated on trying to define the position of Quebec within Canada, and to counter the growing power of the nationalist movement in Quebec. As noted above, they point to official bilingualism, and to one national program after another that seems to work to the disproportionate advantage of Quebec residents. In short, they see a national political agenda dominated by Quebec politicians and the concerns of Quebec, and they see national programs tilted toward the economic advantage of the province. These perceptions were accentuated following the 1993 election when the prime minister and the leader of Her Majesty's Loyal Opposition, both from Quebec, squared off across the floor of the House of Commons. Western Canadians, and quite likely most Canadians outside Quebec, were incredulous that the leader of the Bloc Québécois, Lucien Bouchard, could be leader of the Opposition while still maintaining his ardent commitment to the independence of Quebec and the destruction of Canada as they knew it.

Western Canadian perceptions, it must be admitted, fail to recognize that many Quebecers also see themselves as outsiders to a political system, although in their case one dominated by an anglophone majority. As Braid and Sharpe note:

> Westerners often miss this link, this common alienation that they share with Quebecers, because they perceive that Quebec is firmly inside the national system. The great irony, of course, is that most French Canadians see exactly the opposite; they believe that they are the outsiders, while the vast English-speaking West is part of the power ranged against them.[29]

While Braid and Sharpe may overdraw the parallel, given that objective reality provides somewhat greater support to western perceptions, some provincial leaders in the West have recognized a commonality of interests with the Quebec government. In Alberta, for example, there has been a shared interest in the protection of provincial jurisdiction against intrusions from the federal government and, less consistently, in the greater devolution of federal powers, responsibilities, and fiscal resources. The Alberta government enjoyed a close relationship with Quebec throughout the 1970s and early 1980s, one that was maintained even when the Parti Québécois was in power.[30] However, this perceived commonality of interests was never characteristic of the more general regional political culture, and elite accommodation with Quebec was always engaged in at considerable electoral risk.

The West, incidentally, is not the only region whose residents feel disadvantaged relative to Quebec. In 1993, the Ontario government commissioned a study by Informetrica to compare Ontario's and Quebec's share of federal largesse. Among the findings were the following:[31]

- Quebec received $1.7 billion in net unemployment insurance payments in 1991, while Ontario paid in $900 million more than it received.
- In 1992/93, Quebec had 43 per cent fewer people on welfare than did Ontario, but received 10 per cent more in federal welfare-related transfer payments than did Ontario.

Prime Ministers from Quebec and the West

Since April 1968, three of the six Canadian prime ministers have come from Quebec and three have come from the West. This would suggest a reasonable balance of political influence between the two regions, as would the fact that the office has systematically rotated between the two regions. (It also brings into question the lack of prime ministers from Ontario, but that is another matter!) However, when we examine the length of term served by the six prime ministers, the disparity between the two regions is brought into bold and troubling relief:

| Prime Minister | Region | Time in Office as Prime Minister |
|---|---|---|
| Pierre Trudeau | Quebec | 128 months (April 68 to June 79) |
| Joe Clark | West | 9 months (June 79 to March 80) |
| Pierre Trudeau | Quebec | 52 months (March 80 to June 84) |
| John Turner | West | 3 months (June 84 to Sept 84) |
| Brian Mulroney | Quebec | 105 months (Sept 84 to June 93) |
| Kim Campbell | West | 4 months (June 93 to Nov 93) |
| Jean Chrétien | Quebec | From Nov. 93 to ? |

Two of the three prime ministers from Quebec (Trudeau and Mulroney) held office for a total of 285 months (almost 24 years), compared to a total of 14 months for the three from Western Canada. When one takes into account the open-ended tenure of the current prime minister, the preponderance of Quebec leadership is overwhelming. Prime ministers from the West do little more than provide punctuation marks between extended periods of federal leadership from Quebec.

- In 1992/93, Ontario received 55 per cent of Canada's immigrants and 39 per cent of federal funds for immigration settlement; Quebec received only 19 per cent of the former, but 34 per cent of the latter.

Ontario's campaign for a "fair share" echoes generations of Western Canadian discontent.

The sense that Quebec exercises too much power in national political life is one side of the coin; the other is that the West exercises less than its due. Here it is important to note that Western Canadians are sometimes prone to exaggerate the demographic and economic weight of the West. There is a widespread perception that Western Canada is still the national growth pole, as it was early in the twentieth century, and that the country's demographic and economic centres of gravity are steadily shifting westward. This perception is particularly strong in the two western-most provinces, which have also experienced considerable in-migration from Manitoba and Saskatchewan. Although the underlying reality is that the *regional* shifts in population and economic wealth have been relatively modest, and have in many ways been overshadowed by shifts *among* the four western provinces, this has made little impression on the dominant regional belief that people and money have been moving west while at the same time political power remains firmly entrenched in Quebec. As Figure 5.2 shows, moreover, a significant population gap is now beginning to open up between Quebec and the West, a gap that reflects a decline in Quebec's share of the national population more than growth in the West's share. In 1994, Quebec's share fell below 25 per cent for the first time ever.

It is not surprising, then, that the Charlottetown Accord proposal that Quebec be guaranteed 25 per cent of the seats in the House of Commons in perpetuity met with such strong resistance in the West, and particularly in British Columbia. Arguments that Quebec at that time had 25 per cent of the national population missed the essential point; Western Canadians believe that in relative terms Quebec is shrinking and the West is growing. The Accord's provision was seen as an attempt to lock in a degree of power for Quebec that was already seen as unfair. It is difficult to imagine a constitutional proposal that would have evoked a more hostile response in the West,[32] although a Quebec veto would certainly have been a contender.

The bedrock of Western Canadian discontent is formed by the perception that the Quebec electorate and Quebec politicians exercise too much power in Ottawa and, as a consequence, distort the national agenda and indeed the very definition of the country in ways that work to the disadvantage of the West. This perception enhances regional opposition to constitutional provisions that would recognize the special or distinct status of Quebec, provisions that run counter to the western emphasis on the equality of individuals and provinces. As Figure 5.3 illustrates, opposition to the Charlottetown Accord was greater in the West than it was elsewhere. Although the Accord had elements with considerable appeal to the West, including significant movement on Senate reform, the package as a whole failed to correspond to western constitutional visions. As Alberta premier Ralph Klein said two years later, "I think there's an acknowledgement that traditionally, culturally, and in a language sense, Quebec is somewhat distinct. But in terms of federation, all provinces should be equal."[33]

Western Canadians were more likely than others to mention concessions to Quebec as a major dislike of the Accord (see Box). Yet if they also felt that the Accord had failed to meet Western Canadian expectations, they were not in line with national opinion. In a survey of opinion toward the 1992 constitutional referendum, 55 per cent of the national sample concluded that the Accord had not met Quebec's concerns. However, only 27 per cent felt it had not met the concerns of Western Canadians, compared to 52 per cent who felt that it had not met the concerns of Aboriginal peoples, 50 per cent the con-

FIGURE 5.2   Relative Proportion of the Canadian Population Living in
Quebec and the West

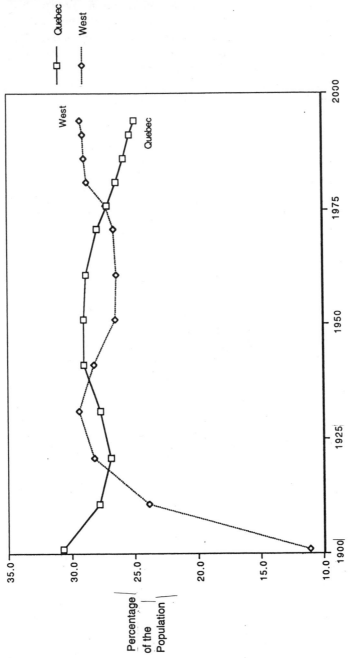

*Source*: Census Canada

FIGURE 5.3   Results of the 1992 Constitutional Referendum

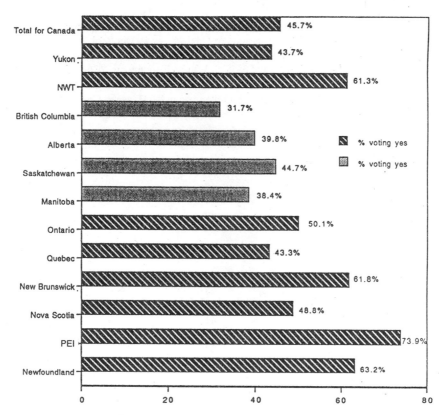

% Voting Yes

*Source*: Elections Canada

Regional Reactions to the Charlottetown Accord

Shortly before the 1992 referendum on the Charlottetown Accord, the Angus Reid Group conducted a national survey of 3,577 respondents, who were asked "which parts of the package do you particularly dislike?" As the following regional breakdown illustrates, Western Canadians were somewhat more likely than others to mention "concessions to Quebec" as elements of the package they particularly disliked. Across the West, 49% mentioned such concessions, compared to 40% of Ontario and 35% of Atlantic respondents. "Concessions to Quebec" were coded to include opposition to the distinct society clause, opposition to Quebec's guarantee of 25% of the seats in the House of Commons, and the more general perception that the package offered "too much for Quebec."

*% mentioning concessions to Quebec as a major dislike of the Charlottetown Accord*

| | |
|---|---|
| British Columbia | 47 |
| Alberta | 54 |
| Saskatchewan | 47 |
| Manitoba | 45 |
| Ontario | 40 |
| Quebec | 5 |
| New Brunswick | 41 |
| Nova Scotia | 28 |
| Prince Edward Island | 24 |
| Newfoundland | 41 |
| | |
| Canada | 34 |

Another 16% of the national respondents, and approximately 15% of those in the West, said that they "hated it all," a reaction that presumably includes "concessions" to Quebec. The survey findings support two important conclusions: that opposition to Quebec's constitutional demands was more pronounced in the West than elsewhere, and that such opposition was by no means unique to the region.

Source: Canada West Foundation, *Public Opinion and the Charlottetown Accord* (Calgary: January 1993), p. 4.

cerns of Ontario, 38 per cent the concerns of Atlantic Canada, and 33 per cent the concerns of women.[34] In the 1992 constitutional referendum study, respondents were asked if they saw the West as a winner in the Charlottetown Accord; 20.4 per cent of Western Canadian respondents did so compared to

25.4 per cent of Ontario respondents, 32.3 per cent of Atlantic respondents, and 34.8 per cent of Quebec respondents.

Western Canadians believe that Quebecers want more constitutional powers for the province of Quebec *and* more power for Quebec within the government of Canada. While they might be prepared to accept a trade-off—special status and enhanced provincial powers for Quebec coupled with diminished Quebec influence in Ottawa—they are not enthusiastic about what is seen to be a general expansion of Quebec's power and influence within the Canadian state. It is the perceived combination of Quebec's dominance of the national political process with the quest for special constitutional status—having their cake and eating it too—that baffles and angers Western Canadians.

In summary, no claim is being made that Western Canadian attitudes toward Quebec, and toward the perceived influence of Quebec in Canadian life, are necessarily unique. To say, for example, that Western Canadians are "baffled and angry" is not to imply that such sentiments are absent elsewhere in the country. Admittedly, some of the underlying dynamics may be unique to the region, but this is not to say that Western Canadians are more extreme in their attitudes than are the residents of Ontario or Atlantic Canada. What may be unique is that in the West these attitudes are woven into distinctive national visions: they are foundational elements in the political culture of the West, and in regional alienation. And perhaps Western Canadian perceptions of Quebec also play a disproportionately important role in shaping more general English-Canadian attitudes toward Quebec. It is in the West that the pull away from the breast-beating anguish and conciliatory attitudes toward Quebec that dominated elite attitudes in English Canada for at least a generation has been greatest.

THE CONTEMPORARY DYNAMICS

As this book is being written, Quebecers are anticipating a referendum on sovereignty before the end of 1995. On one level, this fundamental decision about remaining part of the Canadian federal state is a decision for Quebecers alone to make; they will bear the most immediate costs of that decision and will be its most direct beneficiaries. However, the terms under which Quebec either remains in or leaves Canada are of direct and immediate relevance for all Canadians, including those living in the four western provinces. There is little question that whatever the outcome, the current round of the national unity debate will force Western Canadians to re-examine their position within Canada. The constitutional and institutional foundations of the country will not be left untouched by the Quebec debate, even if the outcome is a decisive rejection of sovereignty.

The Quebec sovereignty debate is of immediate concern and direct relevance for the future of the West in Canada, and as a consequence Western Canadians should be actively involved in it. There is also no doubt that their

Reprinted with permission from Malcolm Mayes, *Edmonton Journal*.

participation could be accompanied by a good deal of anger. Indeed, nothing less should be expected given that the nationalist movement in Quebec threatens to destroy a country that Western Canadians have done so much to build. If Westerners are, at heart, Canadian nationalists rather than being wedded to more narrowly defined regional loyalties, then anger seems an appropriate response to a threat to the country. We should expect, moreover, that such anger would persist should Quebec separate, and that it would play an important role in shaping any negotiations surrounding Quebec's withdrawal. At present, the clearest manifestation of this anger is a growing willingness to endorse Quebec's departure from Canada. An Angus Reid poll conducted in the late spring of 1994, for example, found that 27 per cent of Albertans and 26 per cent of British Columbians agreed that "it would be better in the long run if Quebec were simply to separate from the rest of the country."[35] Western Canadians are also slightly more willing to "play chicken" with Quebec nationalists than are other Canadians. Respondents to a 1991 Gallup survey were asked: "Would you prefer to keep Quebec in Canada by giving it the powers it requests, or should the federal government turn down these requests and risk Quebec separating?" Among British Columbia and Prairie residents, 79 and 78 per cent respectively were prepared to take the risk, compared to 70 per cent of the Ontario respondents and 63 per cent of those from Atlantic Canada.[36]

The anticipated anger of Western Canadians illustrates the pitfalls of any regional participation in the Quebec sovereignty debate. If that anger is expressed, then Western Canadians will be accused of playing into the hands of the separatists. (Sometimes Western Canadians are portrayed as naive in this context, and sometimes they are portrayed as deliberately fostering the breakup of Canada.) But if they smother that anger and reach out to Quebec, it is by no means clear that they will do so to any positive effect. Note, for example, the following comment by Daniel Latouche, one of the most astute interpreters of Quebec for English Canadian readers:

"My Canada includes Quebec." This popular slogan is not only an insult to Quebecers, it adds to the Canadian mystery. Why do English Canadians spend so much time and invest so much energy negating their very existence while insisting on defining themselves through the forceful incorporation of reluctant Quebecers? Can one imagine a Scottish car driver proudly exhibiting a "My Scotland includes Wales" sign in his rear window?[37]

So, when Quebec Liberal leader Daniel Johnson says that it will be up to the rest of Canada to make a "no" vote in the sovereignty referendum meaningful to Quebecers,[38] what should Western Canadians say? There is little question that they would like to make a "no" vote meaningful, but probably not on terms that Mr. Johnson would appreciate.

At the outset of this chapter we suggested that Quebec provides an important regional glue for Western Canada, that regional perspectives have emerged as Western Canadians and their provincial governments have tried to position themselves relative to the constitutional demands of Quebec and Quebec's influence within Ottawa. While it might be going overborad to assert that Quebec has created a regional identity in the West, there is no question that it has played a major role in politicizing those regional attachments which have arisen from other sources. What, then, might happen were Quebec to leave Canada? Would the West dissolve into four disparate provinces in a smaller Canada? Would the status quo prevail? Or would Quebec's departure provide a further regional stimulus to the West, one that might promote new forms of political integration? And what will happen if Quebecers reject any radical solution to their own discontent? Will Quebec continue to serve as a regional glue, as the primary point of reference as Western Canadians position themselves within the national community? To provide a context for these questions, if not necessarily answers, we must turn to a broader discussion of the future of the West.

NOTES

1. Guy Laforest makes the same point from a Québécois nationalist point of view. See *Trudeau and the End of a Canadian Dream* (Montreal & Kingston: McGill-Queen's University Press, 1995).
2. Preston Manning, *The New Canada* (Toronto: Macmillan, 1992), p. 310.
3. The Dominion of Canada purchased the Hudson's Bay Company's land assets in 1868.
4. Cited in Frank H. Underhill, *In Search of Canadian Liberalism* (Toronto: Macmillan, 1960), p. 55.
5. That pattern became more explicit in the Acts of Parliament which created Alberta, Manitoba, and Saskatchewan, and which included minority education guarantees.
6. Roderic Beaujot, *Population Change in Canada: The Challenges of Policy Adaptation* (Toronto: McClelland & Stewart, 1991), p. 296.
7. For a detailed if somewhat polemical look at this period, see John F. Conway, *Debts to Pay: English Canada and Quebec from the Conquest to the Referendum* (Toronto: James Lorimer, 1992), pp. 42 ff.
8. On the other hand, French Canadians were generally higher in the representational pecking order of early provincial governments than were Slavs or Jews.
9. Cited in David E. Smith, *Building A Province: A History of Saskatchewan in Documents* (Saskatoon: Fifth House Publishers, 1992), p. 442.
10. Denis Smith, "Liberals and Conservatives on the Prairies, 1917-1968," in David P. Gagan, ed., *Prairie Perspectives* (Toronto: Holt, Rinehart and Winston, 1970), p. 42.
11. Speech in the House of Commons, June 4, 1973. Cited in Margaret Wente, ed., *I Never Say Anything Provocative* (Toronto: Peter Martin, 1975), p. 113.
12. *Maclean's*, March 29, 1958. Quoted in Wente, ed., *I Never Say*, p. 75.
13. Thomas Van Dusen, *The Chief* (Toronto: McGraw-Hill, 1968), p. 74.
14. Van Dusen, *The Chief*, p. 76.
15. Cited in John Herd Thompson, *The Harvests of War: The Prairie West, 1914-1918* (Toronto: McClelland and Stewart, 1978), p. 137.
16. For example, see J. M. Beck, *Pendulum of Power* (Scarborough: Prentice-Hall, 1968), p.143.
17. See Laforest, *Trudeau and the End of a Canadian Dream.*
18. Cited in Mason Wade, *The French Canadians, 1860-1967*, vol. II (Toronto: Macmillan, 1968), pp. 618-9. It should be noted that the message to stay at home was also delivered by Quebec's religious and political elites who feared the depopulation of the province.
19. *The Gallup Report*, May 20, 1991.

20. Donald V. Smiley, *The Federal Condition in Canada* (Toronto: McGraw-Hill Ryerson, 1987), p. 146.
21. *The Toronto Star*, June 5, 1983, p. F3.
22. Cited in Van Dusen, *The Chief*, p. 112.
23. Paul McKeague, "Preston Manning Poses a Big Threat to Canada," *Gazette* (Montreal), September 26, 1994.
24. Don Braid and Sydney Sharpe, *Breakup: Why the West Feels Left Out of Canada* (Toronto: Key Porter Books, 1990), p. 77. J.F. Conway notes the "continuing francophobia among many westerners." *The West: The History of a Region in Confederation* (Toronto: James Lorimer, 1994), p. 312.
25. For example, see Roger Gibbins, *Prairie Politics and Society: Regionalism in Decline* (Toronto: Butterworths, 1980), p. 179; and Shawn Henry, "Western Alienation Revisited: Political Isolation in Western Canada," unpublished manuscript, University of Calgary, January 11, 1993.
26. We suspect, although we cannot document empirically, that Ontario's power is seen as more legitimate, more proportionate to economic and demographic realities, than is Quebec's, which is not to say that it is resented less.
27. David J. Mitchell, *WAC: Bennett and the Rise of British Columbia* (Vancouver: Douglas & McIntyre, 1983), p. 397.
28. Joe Clark, *A Nation Too Good To Lose* (Toronto: Key Porter Books, 1994), p. 39.
29. Braid and Sharpe, *Breakup*, p. 89.
30. For a more general discussion of this point, see Braid and Sharpe, *Breakup*, Chapter Four.
31. Jeffrey Simpson, "Ontario Begins to Wonder About a Better Deal Within Confederation," *Globe and Mail*, December 1, 1994, p. A22.
32. The 25% seat guarantee is still an issue in Quebec. In April 1995, Quebec Liberal leader Daniel Johnson called for such a condition should constitutional talks resume. Robert McKenzie, "Johnson demands guarantee on MPs," *Gazette* (Montreal), April 5, 1995.
33. Tom Olsen, "Klein calls on Quebec to remain in Canada," *Edmonton Sun*, April 26, 1995.
34. Lawrence LeDuc and Jon H. Pammett, "Referendum Voting: Attitudes and Behaviour in the 1992 Constitutional Referendum," *Canadian Journal of Political Science*, xxviii: 1 (March 1995), p. 20.
35. *Alberta Report*, September 26, 1994, p. 9.
36. *The Gallup Report*, January 24, 1991.
37. Daniel Latouche, "They Just Don't Get It," *Gazette* (Montreal), January 20, 1995.
38. January 18, 1995 speech to the Toronto and Empire Clubs. *Globe and Mail*, January 19, 1995, p. A4.

# CHAPTER SIX

# The Future of the West

As we noted in the introduction to this book, the founding slogan of the Reform Party—"the West wants in!"—provides the best encapsulation to date of nationalist sentiment among Western Canadians, who have sought to play a more vigorous and *effective* role in the life of the country. However, the aspiration for greater inclusion within the national mainstream has been frustrated by the economic and the political organization of Canadian life. Thus Chapter Two identified an extensive litany of regional grievances, some going back to the turn of the century and others as new as the morning paper. Moreover, we saw in Chapter Three that inclusion is not sought on just any terms. Western Canadians have clearly articulated national visions which they have tried to build into Canada's constitutional and institutional framework. Inclusion is the goal, but inclusion on terms that would facilitate regional aspirations and fit the broader fabric of the regional political culture.

Chapter Four explored a variety of ways in which Western Canadians have tried to find a solution to regional grievances. The search has been for an institutional framework within which regional values could find more effective expression and regional interests could be more adequately protected. However, the search has been largely unsuccessful, and thus the structural foundations of western alienation remain in place. While the intensity of that alienation will fluctuate across time and space in response to short-term policy and partisan factors, the sentiment itself will not disappear. In part, this is also because the national visions articulated by Western Canadians rest uneasily within the broader Canadian political culture. More emphatically, they run up against radically different national visions articulated by nationalists and even federalists in Quebec. Therefore, and as Chapter Five explained, the country has reached an uneasy stalemate wherein neither Quebec nor the West is comfortable with the existing set of constitutional and institutional arrangements, but where any move to accommodate the concerns of one region exacerbates tension in the other.

Where, then, does this leave us? Stress continues to characterize the West's relationship within Canada, but is that level of stress a matter of either acute or growing concern? Keep in mind, stress is not necessarily bad. At least for individuals, a reasonable measure of stress is conducive to a healthy and productive life; it provides energy and motivation. But what if the stress is unrelenting? What if the steps taken to ameliorate it fail? And what if new sources of stress appear on the horizon even while the old sources are unabated in their effect? Can stress on the region or within the country become great enough to weaken the national political community to the point where "the West wants in" becomes "the West wants out"?

In raising such questions, we are not trying to be unduly alarmist. After all, Western Canadians have long shown a remarkable endurance for regional stress. The bonds of national unity have been strained on many occasions without threatening the underlying and demonstrably strong commitment of Western Canadians to the national community. It is therefore highly unlikely that western alienation *alone* would be sufficient to make a substantial number of Western Canadians reconsider that commitment. However, the accumulated stress on the country as a whole, most of which stems from the never-ending national unity debate in Quebec, may reach the point where the political system is unable to accommodate additional strain, where a new crisis would inflict serious and perhaps even irreparable damage. Or, it may reach the point where the bonds of national unity erode more slowly but erode nevertheless, causing Western Canadians to drift into a deeper sense of political estrangement. Let us look at these two possibilities in turn.

CATALYSTS FOR CHANGE

In the years to come, as in the years past, the most likely catalyst for change in the Canadian federal state will be the nationalist movement in Quebec. At the extreme, there is no question that the departure of Quebec would constitute a major jolt and an unavoidable catalyst for change. Indeed, it is difficult to imagine that the "rest of Canada" could reconstitute itself as a national community unless it did so within a radically transformed set of federal arrangements, national institutions, and electoral practices. Given that more than half of the remaining Canadian population would live in Ontario, something would have to be done to improve regional representation within Parliament, perhaps through Senate reform, and to fashion an electoral and party system that would bring cleavages other than those based on territory to the fore. If Canadians in this new country were to divide along regional lines of cleavage, it is highly unlikely that a new national community could be forged and sustained.[1] Even if this were avoided, it is by no means certain that Canada would endure, and thus we could be looking at an independent West, or independent parts thereof. However, the fate of the West in the event that Quebec leaves has been addressed elsewhere, and we are prepared to leave the discussion of this somewhat remote possibility to others.[2] Instead, we would like to explore a number of more likely, less dramatic, but still troubling possibilities.

*Renewed constitutional demands from Quebec*

Most Canadians outside Quebec hope and expect that once Quebecers get a chance to make a clear choice on whether Quebec stays in Canada or leaves, they will choose to stay. However, in this eventuality, and perhaps particularly in this eventuality, Canadians would be foolish to expect Quebecers to abandon their quest for a new federal order. A Quebec government, backed by a close "no" vote in a sovereignty referendum, would be in a strong position to advance a transformative constitutional agenda. The prime minister of Canada would still come from Quebec, as would the leader of the Official Opposition, and the threat of another referendum would provide powerful constitutional leverage. Therefore a likely post-referendum scenario is one in which Quebec's demands for a new status *within* Canada escalate and find a receptive audience in Ottawa. As a consequence, it cannot be assumed that the future federal state within which Quebecers would choose to stay would correspond to the western visions sketched in by Chapter Three.

In effect, the price of keeping Quebec in Canada could well be a further estranged West, and this may be a price that many Canadians would be willing to pay. If some region has to lose, it had best be the region that has displayed a dogged commitment to Canada, come what may. What this scenario suggests is an interesting irony, in that the best strategy for the West may be to resist any form of constitutional change for fear that any departure from the status quo would move Canada further from rather than closer to western visions. The irony is that Western Canadians have traditionally been strong advocates for change, but in the future may of necessity form the first line of defence for the institutional and constitutional status quo.

This conclusion may strike some readers as being overly pessimistic, and it is certainly possible that a *decisive* "no" vote in a sovereignty referendum would kill any Quebec constitutional initiatives for a generation to come.[3] It seems more likely, though, that a less-than-decisive "no" will be the outcome, and that such an outcome will touch off another sustained period of constitutional unrest. After all, that is what happened before: Quebec's solid rejection of sovereignty-association in the 1980 referendum led directly to twelve years of constitutional turmoil. Thus the probable future will be one in which Quebec's demands for both formal and informal constitutional change will intensify. In such an environment, it is difficult to imagine an outcome in which the institutions of the Canadian federal state would be brought more into line with the western visions sketched in by Chapter Three. A more likely outcome is one in which Western Canadians feel more and more like Robert Heinlein's "strangers in a strange land." An even more troublesome possibility is that Western Canadians may begin to support the withdrawal of Quebec in the belief that a Canada without Quebec is more likely to be in line with western visions than a Canada that includes Quebec.

## The politics of debt and deficit

Although substantial public debts and deficits are hardly new to Canadians, it has only been in the past few years that they have come to dominate the political agenda for the federal and provincial governments. The mechanics by which this transformation has occurred cannot be addressed within the present context, but there is no question that the champions of debt and deficit reduction have captured the day. But what significance does this have for the West, and for the future of the West in Canada? The significance comes from the fact that provincial governments in the West have adopted a very different approach from that taken by either Ottawa or the provincial governments of Ontario and Quebec. The western provinces have moved aggressively to balance their budgets, and at least to contemplate paying off their debts. Saskatchewan was the first of the four to present a balanced budget in 1995,[4] and it was followed quickly by the other three. Manitoba has gone even further by bringing in legislation that requires balanced budgets every year and a referendum before major tax rates can increase. Saskatchewan and Alberta will likely introduce similar legislation. It should be noted that the provinces have moved along quite different dimensions in addressing the deficit issue: Alberta and Manitoba have relied on expenditure cuts and increases in user fees, Saskatchewan has relied on a mixture of expenditure cuts and tax increases, and British Columbia has used a combination of cuts, tax increases, and creative book-keeping. Yet despite important differences in approach among the four western governments, they appear to have come to the same conclusion. When Saskatchewan's NDP premier Roy Romanow said in a speech to the Saskatoon Chamber of Commerce that "we've got to beat this inherited monster of a debt that is threatening to devour our programs and objectives,"[5] it could well have been Alberta's Progressive Conservative premier Ralph Klein addressing the Edmonton Chamber of Commerce.

But why is this important to an understanding of the future of the West in Canada? To date, the two Central Canadian provinces and the federal government have taken a much more relaxed approach to debts and deficits; the rhetoric of fiscal constraint has been coupled with the continuation of large deficits. As a consequence, the politics of debt and deficit reduction are likely to take on a regional spin. In the wake of their own success in achieving balanced provincial budgets, Western Canadians may come to see the problem as a Central Canadian problem. Ottawa in particular may be seen as a financial albatross draped around the neck of Western Canadians. While this perception would not be entirely new, it could be brought into bold relief by the different track records of the federal and western provincial governments. If Western Canadians come to believe that they will continue to be burdened by an *externally generated* debt, and that the electorates which dominate the federal, Ontario, and Quebec governments will remain insufficiently attentive to the issue, then disengagement from those electorates may come to be seen as the only effective response. In short, the issues of debt and deficits are likely to underscore quite different *regional* perspectives on public finance.

None of this should suggest that Western Canadian voters are wildly out of line with voters elsewhere in the country when it comes to the issue of deficits and debts. However, public concern about these issues is amplified in the West. For example, a Gallup survey conducted in April 1993 asked respondents the following question: "Considering the present economic situation, do you think the federal government should increase spending to stimulate the economy or cut spending to reduce the deficit?"[6] Across the country, 70 per cent opted for a cut in spending compared to 21 per cent who opted for an increase. Across the regions, 64 per cent of Atlantic respondents supported a cut in spending compared to 66 per cent in Quebec and Ontario, 78 per cent on the Prairies, and 80 per cent in British Columbia. A November 1994 Gallup survey found that 63 per cent of British Columbia respondents and 50 per cent of Prairie respondents were "very concerned" about the size of the federal deficit, proportions which compare to 48 per cent in Ontario, 49 per cent in Quebec, and 45 per cent in Atlantic Canada.[7] What remains to be seen is the extent to which regional concerns about the debt and deficit get rolled into the traditional complaints of western alienation.

## The Reform party and the next election

The 1993 election marked a sharp regional break in the Canadian electorate, with the Reform party capturing 51 seats in Western Canada but only a single seat in Ontario. (Reform, however, did place second in 57 Ontario ridings.) In many ways, the election results were ominous for national unity. Not only did they reveal a serious national split, but the Reform party emerged as a powerful regional voice in a Parliament deeply divided along regional and linguistic lines. But what might we expect in the next election? Were the 1993 results an aberration, or should they be seen as a signal of worse to come? Here we are confronted with three very different scenarios for the next election.

In the first, the Liberals maintain their national dominance in the wake of the defeat of the sovereignty referendum in Quebec and a perceived successful attack on the federal deficit. The Reform party pays the price for Liberal success as Canadian voters reject the extremities of Reform's deficit reduction plan, and as the national unity issue recedes in Quebec and across the country. In this scenario, the Liberals hold and perhaps even increase their Western Canadian seats, and Reform is driven back into an Alberta and British Columbia rump. In short, the wave for which Reform has been awaiting fails to arrive, and Reform joins a long list of short-lived regional protest parties.[8] The forces that might have generated the wave, including nationalist unrest in Quebec and an escalating federal deficit, all fade as the federal Liberals establish another sustained period of electoral hegemony. The West, or at least the western West, remains alienated, but a truly national party and government remains in place. Regional unrest smoulders, but the survival of Canada is not threatened as Quebec is back in the fold.

In the second scenario, the Reform party does not collapse but instead succeeds in transforming itself into a national party. Reform not only holds its Western Canadian base but extends its reach into Ontario, at last parlaying its considerable share of the Ontario popular vote into a reasonable number of seats. The Reform wave indeed arrives, but it is a *national* wave, one driven by a neo-conservative agenda informed by political events south of the border, and by the growing unease of English Canadians in the face of escalating constitutional demands from Quebec. Although the wave may not be sufficient to carry Reform into office, it is sufficient to establish Reform as the only national alternative to the Liberals. In this scenario, while the success of Reform means that its role as a champion of regional interests and aspirations is weakened, at the same time issues of particular importance to the West get carried into the national agenda by Reform. Thus the success of Reform means in some real sense that the "West is in," and that the national and regional political agendas have been brought into line.

The third scenario is one in which Reform retains and perhaps even strengthens its western base, but fails to make any significant breakthrough in Ontario or other provinces to the east. In this case, Reform would not be seen as a contender for national office. We might also expect that the regional voice of Reform would become more pronounced, and that Reform supporters may even begin to contemplate a radically different future for the West. This is the scenario that would most likely result if the federal government's constitutional response to Quebec ignores western national visions, if Ottawa's attack on the deficit is half-hearted, and if Reform MPs continue to be assailed as barbarians from the West who are insensitive to the nuances and priorities of national politics.

The general point is that the future of the West cannot be easily disentangled from the future of Reform. While it is not clear which is the chicken and which is the egg, the partisan dynamics of Reform will have considerable bearing on the more general dynamics of regional politics in Canada.

If we step back from the specifics of these catalysts, it may be the case that none by itself has the capacity to rupture the political relationship between the West and the national political community. However, they are unlikely to operate in isolation; regional discontent with respect to one is likely to spill over into the other. The politics of debt and deficit, for example, feed into and are mobilized by the Reform party. Moreover, to the extent that the government in Quebec fails to move aggressively to reduce the provincial deficit, and to the extent that Quebec is singled out as a prime beneficiary of federal spending, then further constitutional demands from Quebec will be seen through the prism of debt and deficit.

THE POLITICS OF DISENGAGEMENT

But what might happen if none of the catalytic events identified above takes place? What would happen if Quebec's nationalist movement and its constitutional demands evaporate, if Canadians from coast to coast applaud Ottawa's efforts to bring federal spending under control, and if the Reform party fades, perhaps in the face of the resurgent Progressive Conservatives who, despite a Quebec-based leader, recapture Western Canadian support? In this scenario, it would be easy to imagine that western alienation would also fade, and that Western Canadians would feel at home within the national community. However, if we retain some grip on political reality, the more likely scenario is the progressive disengagement of Western Canadians from the broader national community. The factors feeding this disengagement are many and varied, but they all work in the same direction to weaken the bonds of national unity. Moreover, the factors which weaken the bonds between the West and the national community will also weaken the bonds among the four western provinces, bonds which in the past have been tenuous at best. In other words, growing estrangement between the West and the rest would not be offset by any growing sense of a regional community stretching from Manitoba to the Pacific coast. To the contrary, linkages among the four western provinces are unlikely to be revitalized by any of the catalytic events identified above.

In Chapter Five, we argued that Quebec provides part of the regional glue for Western Canada, that the West as a *political* region is brought into being by and sustained as a counterpoint to the constitutional demands of Quebec. We would now make this argument in even broader terms by suggesting that *Canada provides the glue for the West, and that whatever weakens the national community is likely to weaken regional ties within Western Canada.* As the federal government moves to scale back direct financial involvement in social programs, as national standards are weakened in the attempt to accommodate not only fiscal pressures but also constitutional pressures emanating from Quebec, as Ottawa becomes increasingly irrelevant to economic management in the face of continental free trade and globalization, then the federal government *and Canada* will become less relevant for those living in the four western provinces. However, if the national glue weakens, so too will weaken any sense of regional community among the four western provinces. The individual provinces will be more likely to plot their own courses, and to position themselves as best they can in the new context of continental free trade and a global economy. For example, there is no reason to expect that as the relevance of Ottawa and the federal government decreases for British Columbians, they will suddenly discover a new sense of regional kinship with the residents of the Prairie provinces. They are at least as likely to discover a new sense of kinship with American states in the Pacific Northwest, a kinship already embodied in the recent emergence of "Cascadia."

We are left, then, with the conclusion that any further deterioration in national unity is unlikely to lead to a transformation of "the West wants in" to "the West wants out." A more likely one, but an equally distressing outcome, is that the West will dissolve as a political region in lockstep with the weakening of Canada as a national community. Should this happen, the progressive disengagement of at least British Columbia from the region would be all but certain. In a new global environment, Western Canadians will look more and more to their provincial communities as their emotional ballast in the challenging seas of international trade and globalization. Therefore while "the West" may not want out, some of its component communities may want precisely that.

Western Canadians have always believed in a strong, national community. A Canada that has been gutted of any clear sense of collective purpose, that has been radically decentralized in the effort to appease nationalist forces within Quebec, and that no longer has the financial resources or political will to pursue national social programs—such a Canada would be of limited interest to Western Canadians. Unfortunately, in that case neither would the West itself be of continued interest to the people who live there.

NOTES

1. For an elaboration of this line of thought, see Roger Gibbins, "Speculations on a Canada Without Quebec," in Kenneth McRoberts and Patrick Monahan, eds., *The Charlottetown Accord, the Referendum, and the Future of Canada* (Toronto: University of Toronto Press, 1993), pp. 264-73.
2. For a thorough and insightful discussion of the West in a Canada without Quebec, see Gordon Gibson, *Plan B: The Future of the Rest of Canada* (Vancouver: The Fraser Institute, 1994).
3. A decisive "no" vote would be one in which less than 40% of the Quebec electorate endorsed the sovereignty option in a provincial referendum. This would mean that the pro-sovereignty vote was less than the pro-sovereignty-association vote in 1980.
4. It should be noted that in many respects, New Brunswick has been the leading province in addressing the problems of debt and deficit reduction. However, and as is usually the case, events in Atlantic Canada are likely to have minimal perceptual penetration in the West.
5. *Star-Phoenix* (Saskatoon), January 16, 1993.
6. *The Gallup Report*, April 24, 1993.
7. *The Gallup Poll*, December 5, 1994.
8. For a much more detailed discussion of the future prospects for Reform, see Tom Flanagan, *Waiting for the Wave: The Reform Party and Preston Manning* (Toronto: Stoddart, 1995).

# Index